Medieval Art

Medieval Art

An Introduction to the Art and Architecture of Europe, A.D. 300 - A.D. 1300

Norris Kelly Smith, Ph.D.

*Professor of the History of Art,
Washington University, St. Louis*

P- 74

WM. C. BROWN COMPANY PUBLISHERS
Dubuque, Iowa

ART HORIZONS SERIES

Consulting Editor

WILLARD F. WANKELMAN
Bowling Green State University

A *growing interest in art and art history is evident today in the United States and has created a need for a new approach in the formulation of classroom teaching materials.*

The ART HORIZONS SERIES, *designed for introductory courses in art appreciation and art history, transmits the excitement of the subject to the student seeking a liberal education. This series offers both the student and teacher flexibility of subject matter as well as authoritative writing in each topic area. Although the individual titles are self-contained, collectively they cover the major subjects usually discussed in an introductory course.*

preface

While I have written this treatise in the hope that it will prove useful to undergraduate students in both introductory and intermediate courses in art history, I hesitate to call it a textbook. For me, at least, that word suggests an orderly compend or digest of basic information; and this book is not that. It would have been easy to write such a work— especially so in the field of medieval art; but I am not persuaded that a student should spend his time reading textbooks of that sort.

From the beginning the academic discipline of art history has faced difficult and still largely unresolved problems as to the nature of its purposes and of its methodology. At first there was art appreciation. That is essentially what Ruskin taught, as Slade Professor at Oxford: instead of dispensing well-documented information *about* works of art, he unabashedly expounded the elements of beauty and truth which he found revealed in the works themselves. Since the 1860s, however, our conceptions both of art and of higher learning have changed: in their different ways, both activities have become more inbred, more nearly self-justifying. Like Manet and his followers, the scholars of the later nineteenth century could not abide the moralistic subjectivism of Ruskin's generation. Under the impact of the burgeoning sciences, we may suppose, and especially of the biological sciences, which had lately achieved such conspicuous success in devising systems of classification and in defining broad principles of evolutionary and genetic development, the art historian devoted himself increasingly to the systematic and objective tasks of identifying and classifying a vast number of previously unstudied works and at times even attempted (as in Wolfflin's *Principles of Art History*) to define universal laws of evolutionary change in matters of style.

Because of their relatively uncharged character and anonymous provenance, works of medieval art have lent themselves especially well to being classified according to period, region, and school, and to being linked in genetic *stemmae*. During the past two hundred years an admirable amount of scholarly effort has been devoted to making manageable the immense body of material that has come down to us from the Middle Ages; and yet most of that labor has been quite external to the works of art themselves, being directed toward solving problems of dating, origin, and interrelationship rather than toward the explication of matters that would have seemed meaningful or important to the artists who actually produced the works in question. When one has distinguished the class of Burgundian Romanesque churches from all other classes of churches, or when one has successfully identified all the manuscripts that were produced in the Palace School at Aachen, one has not thereby come one step closer to understanding the sense or meaning of a single Burgundian church or Carolingian manuscript painting. What one *has* done, of course, is to prepare the way for giving a rigorous slide test at the end of a college course in medieval art. There are times when the academic enterprise does seem astonishingly inbred!

In the chapters that follow I have tried insofar as possible to confine myself to a discussion of matters that the artists themselves would have thought relevant to their motivating concerns—though of course they would have been no more inclined than a modern painter would be to express such ideas verbally. I was introduced to the study of medieval art in these terms nearly thirty years ago by Meyer Schapiro, to whom I readily acknowledge a great indebtedness. After twenty years of teaching, I am no longer able always to say what specific ideas I should attribute to him. There are probably more of them than I have explicitly acknowledged.

contents

1

Early Christian Art

*Rome (7) Ravenna (1)
8 illustration*

Medieval art is mainly the art of the Christian church. This is not to say, however, that it is essentially Christian, for it would have seemed as strange to Peter and Paul as it does to many of us today. Its various styles were not determined by tenets of Christian faith, and much of its content would have been found offensive both by the saints of the early church and by the reformers of the sixteenth century. Though it should by no means be regarded as an expression of the "life" of the Middle Ages (no art is so comprehensive or so reportorial as that), it addressed, and was conditioned by, a succession of historical and cultural situations so different from those in which either Paul or Calvin lived that it inevitably spoke in terms they would have found uncongenial, if not "unchristian."

So far as we know, the earliest Christians had no visual art. There was good reason why this should have been the case. For one thing, the second of the Ten Commandments forbids the making of an "image or likeness of anything that is in heaven above, or that is in the earth beneath, or that is in the water under the earth." Though the commandment was no longer strictly observed by the Jews of the Roman world, it was bound up with a way of thinking that pervades the whole Bible. Any reader of that book will have been struck by the fact that one never encounters in the Bible, except perhaps in the Book of Revelation at the very end of the New Testament, a description of the visual appearance of anything—man, beast, object, or scene. Biblical writers were not interested in the act of observing; they could never have become scientists. It was, rather, the Greeks who examined the world and analyzed its anatomy, with an objectivity that is equally evident in the sculpture of Polyclitus and the writings of Aristotle. But the Greeks found Paul's preaching "foolishness," for it dealt with an order of

1

things that not only was invisible but seemed to contradict or negate the very conception of reality on which they relied.

To the extent that the earliest Christians shared the apostle's sense of the irremediable opposition between Biblical and Greek thought, they drew back from the conventional imagery of the largely Greek-speaking Mediterranean world. As the writers of the early church long declared, the only image that mattered was to be found in the believer's likeness to Christ. Statues and temples, they said, were the instruments of pagan idolatry—of a worship that was tainted and encumbered with *things*. They probably felt, as some modern artists feel, that the sculptural or sculpturesque image of the body tends to equate persons with objects, an equation they found intolerable.

Yet the art that Moses had had in mind, of course, was that of Egypt, which, like the classical art of Greece, was reductive and impersonal, stressing the objective reality of types and of conceptual schemata at the expense of all that pertains to the passionate experience of living persons. The Roman art of Paul's day, on the other hand, was far more personal than that. Such sculpture as there was was in good part devoted to an individualizing kind of portraiture; the Romans had little taste for creating objective abstractions of the kind we see in the works of Polyclitus. More important than sculpture was painting— especially landscape painting, at the core of which there lies always the experience of an observer who stands as a fully self-conscious person at the center of his world. The old Homeric and Hesiodic themes were giving way to a new subject matter in which pastoral, idyllic, and garden-like scenes were prominent, as well as whimsical and fantastic inventions of a kind that greatly offended the conservative architect Vitruvius because they were so contrary to his old-fashioned and hardheadedly Roman sense of the matter-of-fact reality of things. Along with changes in subject matter came changes in style: Roman artists depended increasingly, as time went on, upon effects of light, color, and touch, and were less and less concerned with the clear definition of objects and with their placement in a coherent spatial setting. The somewhat alienated citizen, who was no longer asked by the autocratic imperial state to play the part of a Cincinnatus or an Horatius, was inclined to retreat, it would seem, from the arena of military and political affairs into a world of reverie and imagination. Mystery religions, promising personal salvation from death, were more attractive to many people than was the state-sponsored worship of the old gods.

Some of those people were Christian—but first of all they had been Roman. Just as American Christians draw most of their civilizing habits and conventions not from the church but from their American background and milieu, so the Christians in Rome brought into the life of the church many of the unspoken presuppositions and unexamined attitudes of the Roman populace. By the middle of the second century it no longer seemed inappropriate to make pictures of Biblical subjects. The Romans were probably as accustomed as we are to reading illustrated books and to seeing easel paintings and frescoes that dealt with narrative themes. Their conversion to the Christian faith could not have eradicated that essentially visualizing orientation that was deeply engrained in Graeco-Roman thought.

The earliest works of Christian art that have survived are the wall paintings in the catacombs. The latter are vast networks of tunnels outside the walls of Rome—passageways cut from the soft rock underlying the region and used by the Roman community at large, in keeping with a tradition of underground burial that went back at least to Etruscan times. By the beginning of the third century it was not uncommon for the more prosperous Christian families to have chapel-like burial chambers prepared for their use in the catacombs—little *cubicula,* the walls of which were frequently decorated in the light, impressionistic manner that was fashionable at the time for the embellishment of domestic interiors. Within the over-all scheme were set little scenes illustrating God's power to save his people: Noah in his ark, Daniel in the lions' den, the three Israelites in Nebuchadnezzar's fiery furnace, Moses striking the rock to bring forth water in the wilderness (a reference to the saving waters of baptism), the raising of Lazarus, and other such subjects.

These are not works of medieval art, but they are perhaps indicative of that change of outlook that would in the long run cause the Roman state to fail and would make possible the rise of the medieval church. They are colorful little pictures that reveal to us the highly personal conceptions of salvation and of blessedness with which the cosmopolitan Christians of the Roman capital were preoccupied. Noah, for instance, is not represented as the navigator of a ship that bore the progenitors of all later animals and men; he stands alone in a little box,

Figure 1. *The Story of Jonah.* Catacomb painting, Rome, ca. 250. (Courtesy of Dr. Franz Stoedtner, Düsseldorf.)

lifting his arms in prayerful thanksgiving for his solitary salvation. The most popular of all such themes was probably the story of Jonah (Fig. 1). However, we are not shown the willful, reluctant, and sulky missionary we read of in the Old Testament; instead, we see Jonah being saved from the sea (a favorite symbol, in the ancient world, of the flux and precariousness of existence) and Jonah reclining at ease under his gourd vine, enjoying the serenity of a garden paradise. Non-Christian Romans found similar satisfaction in images of the sleeping Endymion, of idyllic pastoral scenes, and of figures floating upward in a spacious void. In all such subjects there is expressed an attitude of disengagement from the political and historical world that is in some ways similar to what we see in the French Impressionism of the 1870s and '80s (a movement that again was indicative of a change of attitude that would shortly make it impossible for Europe to maintain its imperialistic hegemony over the rest of the world).

During the third century the situation changed. The peace and stability Rome had enjoyed under the five Antonine emperors broke down: the economy deteriorated; the army, now largely composed of non-Roman provincials, was ill paid and rebellious, often using its power to install and to depose emperors at its whim; the frontiers of the empire were harried by its enemies in both the north and the east. Toward the end of the century the decline was temporarily checked by Diocletian (284-305), who reformed the administration by dividing and subdividing the empire and by establishing a hierarchy of deputies to govern these divisions, and who introduced into his court the oriental patterns of ceremonious ritual and of splendid ceremonial dress that were to remain characteristic of life at the centers of power, both civil and ecclesiastical, throughout the Middle Ages.

As the prestige of the Roman state declined, that of the church increased—possibly because membership in the church could fulfill a need for something the state was less and less able to provide. For during this time the nature of the church changed, also. The more or less autonomous local groups of ecstatic believers we read of in the book of The Acts of the Apostles—persons who were given on occasion to "speaking in tongues" and who gathered informally in order to eat and to sing together in love feasts—were gradually transformed in the second and third centuries into a well-organized and increasingly liturgical church, complete with an ordained, professional clergy and, by the end of that period, with the rudiments of an ecclesiastical architecture. Despite sporadic persecution at the hands of the state, the church had managed to establish itself as an institution of major importance.

The last severe persecutions took place during the final year or two of Diocletian's reign. The emperor's first edict against the Christians stipulated that "the churches should be levelled with the ground and the scriptures destroyed with fire. . . ." It was efficiently carried out; nothing remains of the church buildings, which, according to Eusebius, were numerous at that time. In the long run the persecution proved unrewarding, however, so that by the year 311, even the implacable Galerius (Diocletian's son-in-law and his "Caesar" in the East) thought it wise to publish an edict of religious toleration. After Diocletian's abrupt abdication in 305, there was political confusion in the West for seven years, or until Constantine won the throne in 312. In the following year he and Licinius are said to have issued their celebrated Edict of Milan, permitting all to worship as they saw fit. After defeating Licinius in 323 and making himself sole Augustus, Constantine took steps to put Christianity on equal footing with paganism, even going so far as to provide partial tax support for the church.

It is at this point, when the leader of the state had appointed the church to a semi-official position, and when the leaders of the church (who had once so vehemently opposed the claims of the state and had denounced its emperor as antichrist) had decided to accept not only that status but financial aid from the state, that one may perhaps mark the beginning of the Middle Ages; for there is no more important factor in the make-up of medieval civilization than the alliance of church and state that was initiated by Constantine and fully established in the 390s by Theodosius. From this point onward the church undertook to uphold and to defend the imperial state, to which its own structure was increasingly assimilated as time went on.

The nature of Constantine's motivations has been debated for generations. He was probably a genuine convert to Christianity, though he was baptized only on his deathbed in 337; yet it could hardly have been otherwise, since the church could not have accepted in those days a member who wore the royal purple and required others to prostrate themselves before him. The early church was conspicuous among Roman institutions for its equalitarianism; to its members the imperial trappings would have smacked still of the cult of the deified ruler. Yet Constantine himself appears to have been uncertain as to how he should play the part of Emperor. Into his triumphal arch (312-315) he had incorporated eighteen large reliefs that had been removed from imperial monuments of the first and second centuries. In each of these one sees the emperor (addressing his legionaries, making offerings of incense, hunting), and in every panel he is shown in a casual *con-*

trapposto pose, is dressed in the simple tunic of a Roman citizen, and is grouped with other figures in varied and informal compositions. In all eighteen, that is, there is preserved the image of the emperor as "first citizen" (in the manner of Augustus) rather than as godlike potentate (in the manner of Diocletian). However, in the two north-face reliefs that depict the *oratio* and the *liberalitas* of Constantine's triumph of 312, the emperor is presented frontally, as the central figure in a symmetrical group of courtiers. In the second of these, in fact, he is seated on a high throne while the members of his court stand on either side, turn toward him, and raise their right hands in what amounts already to a medieval oath of fealty (Fig. 2).

The matter is important, for it bears upon one of the first decisions that the emperor and his bishops had to make. Now that the church had become a semi-official agency of the state, it needed for the first

Figure 2. Reliefs from the Arch of Constantine, (Rome) 312-315. (Photo Alinari, Florence.)

time not just assembly halls but Architecture. It needed visible symbols, that is, of its permanent possession of an important place in the fabric of the city of Rome and of the Roman state. Already in the third century the church had erected longitudinal buildings to house its now liturgical services. We know nothing about them in detail, but we may reasonably suppose that they were as far from being imposing works of architectural art as are the "kingdom halls" of the Jehovah's Witnesses—a present-day Christian group that opposes the pretensions of the American state (and sometimes suffers persecution for doing so) much as the earliest Christians rejected the ultimate claims of Rome. Axiomatically, institutions that are opposed to the state and its culture have no need for the art of architecture, which is peculiarly the art of *established* institutions. All was changed, however, once the bishops had joined hands with the emperor. Now they could draw funds from the state treasury in order to build structures that would attest to the church's new status as just such an institution.

But what form should they take? Constantine had just brought to completion a great public hall in the Forum—the Basilica Nova, that had been begun by his rival, Maxentius, between 305 and 310. It was an immense arcuated and vaulted edifice, its central space flanked on either side by four huge columns, each nearly 65 feet high. It had an apse at one end for the magistrates; with minor modifications it would have made a thoroughly satisfactory church. But apparently the bishops had no interest in imperialistic grandeur of this sort. Though the Constantinian Church of St. Peter (dedicated in 326 and demolished in the sixteenth century) was a much larger building than the Basilica of Maxentius, it was less imposing, being based on earlier and less pretentious prototypes. In fact, it was almost the same size as, and similar in form to, the Basilica Ulpia, a law courts building that had been erected by the Emperor Trajan around A.D. 110 and that, in turn, was related to still earlier public buildings in a tradition reaching back to pre-Augustan times.

In other words, what the bishops and the emperor decided to build, once they had resolved upon providing the church with an architecture commensurate with that of other Roman institutions, was essentially a republican hall, in defense of that image of civil authority that is set forth in the Flavian reliefs on the Arch of Constantine. It must have struck the Emperor that, in the midst of socio-political deterioration, the members of the Christian church still practiced, by and large, the ancient Roman virtues of loyalty, courage, devotion to duty, and frugal austerity; and it may well have occurred to him that if only he could propagate Christianity throughout the Empire, he might be able to check its decay and to restore to the life of the state something of the old integrity that had made it possible for the Romans to rule the world in centuries past. Wherefore he helped his churchmen to build a great hall which, though it was the second largest room in Rome (surpassed only by the Basilica Ulpia), was yet composed of a large number of relatively small elements (Fig. 3). There were nearly a

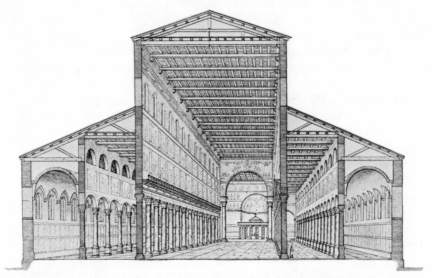

Figure 3. Perspective restoration of interior, Old. St. Peter's Church, Rome, ca. 325. (Courtesy of Dr. Franz Stoedtner, Düsseldorf.)

hundred columns standing on the floor of the church, and there were many small windows at the clearstory level. The connections among the architectural members were not stressed, as they later would be in Romanesque and Gothic buildings; elements were joined into groups mainly by their being seen to stand side by side in close succession. The space was large and orderly, making it easy for the worshiper to comprehend the structure of the building and his position within it.

One did not enter the church directly from the street. In front of the building was an atrium—that is, an open garden surrounded by walls and by a roofed walkway, or loggia, in the midst of which there was probably a well or fountain at which the faithful performed ablutions before entering the church itself. After leaving the secular city and passing through that preparatory garden space, the baptized and instructed believer could enter the great nave, which was nearly 300 feet long. Its walls were richly decorated with paintings or mosaics and with polished marbles, its flat wooden ceiling was probably gilded, its floor was inlaid with colorful geometrical patterns, its windows were filled with stone grilles that admitted daylight in little pinpricks so as to make the vast interior shadowy and awesome. The congregation stood in the nave (there were no chairs or pews) and faced the apse, in the center of which was a small altar, and behind that the bishop's throne, with benches at either side for the deacons and presbyters. In performing the eucharistic liturgy, the priest stood behind the altar table and faced the congregation.

What happened inside such a church had little to do with the ecstatic (glossolalia) of the earliest converts; it stressed, instead, the necessity of lawful community, of orderly participation within an organized society. Here the believer made manifest his citizenship in the company of God's people, his submission to a collective order, now so Roman in form, that stood over against the muddled uncertainty of the world. Even as Plato had banished the poets and musicians from his Republic, so ecstasy was banished in the interest of stability and decorum.

We should not be surprised, then, to discover that the Christian art of the mid fourth century was markedly classicistic in nature. One of the best examples of the style is to be found in the sarcophagus of one Junius Bassus (died 359), the principal face of which is decorated with ten groups of Biblical figures, all of which are clearly Hellenic in form and pose (Fig. 4). On the upper level the groups are enframed by columns in such a way that one can easily imagine that the events are taking place in the aisle of a basilican church such as Old St. Peter's. Although there is some tendency toward diagrammatic schematization (as in the grouping of Adam and Eve or of Daniel and his lions), and though the figures are somewhat stubby (as in the fourth-century reliefs on the Arch of Constantine), the over-all effect is reminiscent of the Flavian style to which Constantine himself was attracted. The purposes of the Christian leaders of that era were perhaps not so different from those of the Emperor Julian the Apostate (361-363) as we have sometimes been led to believe. The revival of the old standards of Roman decorum was evidently sought by Christian and non-Christian alike.

As it turned out, however, neither Julian's efforts to reinstate paganism nor Christian efforts to resuscitate a republican spirit could check the decline of Rome's fortunes. The state did not grow into the likeness of the early church; instead, the church patterned itself increasingly after the autocratic court. By the beginning of the fifth century it was

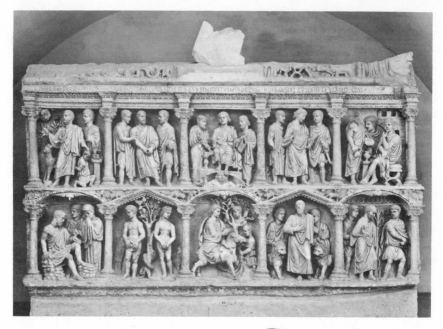

Figure 4. Sarcophagus of Junius Bassus, (Rome) ca. 359. Grottoes of St. Peter's Basilica, Vatican City. (Photo courtesy of Hirmer Fotoarchiv München.)

Constantine's own image of imperium (in contrast to that of the Flavian and Hadrianic reliefs) that had carried the day. We can see this in one of the oldest surviving works of Christian art in the new state-sponsoring vein—namely, the mosaic in the flattened apse of the little church of Sta. Pudenziana in Rome (Fig. 5). The image was probably installed shortly before the sack of Rome by the Visigoths in 410.

Although the mosaic has been extensively and badly restored, especially in the lower right section, one can make out what the form of the original invention must have been. The figure of Christ, dressed as an emperor and enthroned before the Heavenly Jerusalem, was shown to be attended by a courtly gathering of apostles, each of whom raised his right hand toward his Lord, even as Constantine's courtiers had done, in keeping with the ceremonious practices that had been introduced by Diocletian. No longer do we see the beardless young Christ of the catacomb paintings; he has become the bearded, mature figure we are familiar with in later art, a governing magistrate on his apsidal throne rather than a shepherd boy in a landscape.

Yet there is preserved in the mosaic much of the spatial depth, rotund modeling, and freedom of gesture that were characteristic of earlier Roman painting. The figures in the foreground are cut off by the frame, thereby implying that the scene is spatially continuous behind and beyond the frame; light shimmers on the roof tiles of the loggia in the middle distance; and the buildings of the heavenly city stand out against a colorful sky much as do buildings in Pompeian wall decorations of the first century. On the other hand, there appear in the sky the four beasts of the Apocalypse (Rev. 4 : 7), which were taken by the early church to be symbols of the four Evangelists, Matthew, Mark, Luke, and John. Symbolism of this kind is of the greatest importance in medieval thought; one encounters it in countless heraldic devices, emblems, and diagrammatic groupings, as we shall see. It seems incongruous, however, in the still optical or landscape-like imagery of the Sta. Pudenziana mosaic. The work has one foot in antiquity and the other in the Middle Ages.

When Alaric's Visigoths invaded Rome in 410, the imperial court had already been removed from that city to Ravenna, in northeastern

Figure 5. Apsidal mosaic, Sta. Pudenziana, Rome ca. 400. (Courtesy of Dr. Franz Stoedtner, Düsseldorf.)

Italy; and it was in Ravenna that Romulus Augustulus, the last of the emperors in the west, was deposed by the Germanic chieftain Odoacer, in 476. With the departure of the leaders of the state, it devolved upon the church to assume a new measure of responsibility for the maintenance of civil order in the former capital and, in general, throughout the disintegrating empire. In 413, St. Augustine, bishop of Hippo in North Africa, was inspired by the sack of Rome to begin work on his *City of God* (*De Civitate Dei*), in which he contrasted the ideal polity of God's church with the corruption of the "city of the world," and thereby laid the foundations, whether intentionally or not, for that medieval conception of the role of the church that would eventually make it an imperial institution in active competition at times with the secular monarchy.

St. Augustine died in 430. The following year saw the accession of Pope Sixtus III, under whom there was erected, in the church of Sta. Maria Maggiore, an impressive symbol of episcopal authority in Rome (Fig. 6). Its architectural style is of such classic purity as to have given rise to the unfounded contention that the building must

Figure 6. Perspective restoration of interior, Sta. Maria Maggiore, Rome, ca. 435. (From: G. Dehio & G. von Bezold, *Die Kirchliche Baukunst des Abendlandes*, Stuttgart, 1884-1901.)

have been a civil basilica of earlier date which was converted to ecclesiastical use only in the 430s. Yet obviously its formal sobriety is
perfectly in keeping with the purpose of the church at the time, which
was to combat the moral and spiritual laxity that had made the capital
so vulnerable to barbarian conquest.

Along the nave walls of Sta. Maria Maggiore—down the left side
and up the right—runs a series of mosaics illustrating episodes from the
first six books of the Old Testament. For the most part, the subjects
were selected in order to demonstrate the primacy of the sacred over
the secular, of the church over the state, or of the people of God over
their enemies. Unlike the catacomb paintings of earlier days, these images are collective and institutional in reference rather than personal
or individualistic. For instance, we see Abraham, as a civil leader at
the head of his military retinue, making submission to the priest-king
Melchizedek, who offers him bread and wine (Gen. 14 : 18), the elements of the Eucharist. Or again, Abraham and Isaac are shown turning
toward a temple-like building on their right, while Lot and his nefarious
daughters turn left toward the city of Sodom—the "city of the world"
that was doomed to destruction. We see Moses and the Israelites safely
beyond the Red Sea, while Pharaoh and his army, coming forth from
another godless city, are swept to their death in the waters (cf. Jonah).
Farther along, the walls of Jericho come tumbling down as Joshua's army
marches to triumph with its Ark. What is argued, it would seem, is that
the fall of Rome to the Visigoths (who were, by the way, Christian,
though of the Arian persuasion) was a just punishment visited on the
city for its wickedness, of which St. Augustine gives us a good description in his *Confessions*. The mosaics declare that the history of the
people of God is as long and as heroic as that of Rome itself—that
God's power has proved itself effective in the world against those
persons and nations who have opposed him.

In style, the mosaics tend toward a flattened, schematic kind of
composition, as we plainly see in *The Parting of Abraham and Lot*
(Fig. 7). It was not the story of Abraham's life that mattered to the
artist; as a "character" Abraham is indistinguishable from Lot, and he
does not occupy the kind of stage-space in which we could imagine
his moving freely or acting effectively. What mattered was the choice
between good and evil, or between the *Civitas Dei* and the *Civitas
terrena*. Such ideas may be illustrated by narrative events, but the
events are wholly subsidiary to the ideas. The extent of the artist's
departure from the older ways of thinking may best be gauged by
examining the lower section of the image in question, which is given
over to a pastoral landscape, complete with rocks, vegetation, and tiny

Figure 7. *Parting of Abraham and Lot.* Mosaic, Sta. Maria Maggiore, ca. 435. (Courtesy of Dr. Franz Stoedtner, Düsseldorf.)

figures of men and of animals. It serves to fill space and to indicate that Abraham and Lot were shepherds, but its jumbled and meaningless composition stands in sharpest contrast to the imposing and emblematic symmetry of the upper section. Clearly the artist had no interest whatever in the old meanings of idyllic landscape painting. Moreover, it is in the nature of mosaic as a medium that it minimizes the element of optical verisimilitude in the rendering of a scene, thereby making it difficult for the observer to identify himself with the figures, or his world with their world. The mosaic lies flat and glistening on the wall itself; it is not a "window" opening upon a spatial and atmospheric vista.

Rome was sacked again in 455 by Gaiseric's Vandals, was captured once more by the German Ricimer in 462, and was largely depopulated in the course of its long besiegement by Belisarius in the 530s. With these successive blows, the city ceased to be a major center of artistic activity, yielding place to Ravenna and especially to Constantinople. In the former city basilican churches were erected both by the Roman emperors and by the Ostrogothic king Theodoric the Great, who seized the throne in 493 and ruled over an Italian kingdom as best he could until his death in 526. A building that dates from Theodoric's reign is the Church of San Apollinare Nuovo—similar in form and in name to another church, that of San Apollinare in Classe, which was erected shortly afterward in what was then the port town of Classis, about three miles outside the walls of Ravenna. These are comparatively small basilicas, without transepts, which owe their distinction chiefly to their splendid mosaic decorations, which were installed in the mid sixth century after the city had been recaptured for Justinian by Belisarius.

Let us consider only one of the mosaic panels from the cycle that adorns the upper walls of San Apollinare Nuovo—the image of the *Miracle of the Loaves and Fishes* (Fig. 8). We see at once that the scene has now been removed from the world of historical event far

Figure 8. *Miracle of the Loaves and Fishes.* Mosaic, San Apollinare Nuovo, Ravenna, ca. 545. (Courtesy of Dr. Franz Stoedtner, Düsseldorf.)

more radically than was the case in Sta. Maria Maggiore. As it is re-counted in the Gospel of Matthew, the episode involved the gathering of some five thousand people on the hills above the Sea of Galilee and the distribution of an immense quantity of food among them. In the mosaic, however, there are only five persons, arranged as though par-ticipating in a solemn liturgy like that of the mass. They are placed, not against the sky but against a continuous field of luminous gold, in one of the earliest appearances of what was to remain a favorite setting for sacred figures in later medieval art. The mosaicist no longer cares about men's capacity for purposeful action in space and time; his figures are expressionless, their ritual gestures are wholly undramatic. By now we have passed beyond the realm of Early Christian art and into that of the Byzantine.

FOOTNOTES

[1]William MacDonald makes the interesting observation that one of the ances-tors of the Christian basilica is to be found in a small basilican building that served as a throne room on the Palatine Hill in Rome. It was built around A.D. 85 by one of the Flavian emperors—an affirmation, we may suppose, of just the concep-tion of rulership that is proclaimed in the above-mentioned reliefs.

2

Byzantine Art

Scarcely less important than his appointment of the church to an official status was Constantine's decision to remove the seat of imperial government in A.D. 330 to a New Rome that he caused to be built on the site of the little city of Byzantium, a seaport on the Bosporus that had been founded by Greek traders nearly a thousand years earlier. The idea of an eastern capital was not a new one; Diocletian had based his government in Nicomedia, in recognition of the fact that the empire's economic center of gravity lay among its great cities, all of which were at the eastern end of the Mediterranean, and that the religio-political ideas that emanated from the East seemed especially compelling at that point—witness his orientalization of the imperial court. As Rome declined, then, there arose in Constantinople a city of legendary splendor which, alone among all the cities of the Roman Empire, remained an urbane metropolis throughout the Middle Ages— The City, as it was called, where reigned a continuous line of Roman emperors until the last of them was killed by the Turks in 1453.

Yet from the fact that this city alone survived the successive onslaughts of Persian, Slav, and Saracen, one would surmise, and rightly enough, that its position was generally a defensive one. Despite its sophistication, its art and life belong to that long interregnum we call the Middle Age; for though the Byzantine artist was never out of touch with the artistic traditions of classical antiquity, he was almost as remote as a Celtic monk from the secular and cosmopolitan orientation of that earlier era. While he returned periodically to its art for fresh inspiration, and though he kept alive (albeit in a state of suspended animation) those forms and ideas which, when reanimated, would give rise to the art of the Italian Renaissance, he worked within conventional limits that were almost as narrow, and that had as little to

17

do with direct observation of the visible world, as those of pharaonic Egypt. What came to the fore in medieval Byzantium, one might say, was the Egyptoid aspect of classical Greek thought. In Plato's conservative doctrine of the ultimate and timeless reality of forms and ideas, in his preoccupation with types and norms rather than with stubborn particulars, in his mythopoeic and nonhistorical attitude toward the state, in his indifference toward the world of contemporaneous event, in his notion that there is a succession of hierarchical stages ascending from the mundane toward the divine (or, in Byzantine thought, descending from the divine to the mundane), in his devotion to moderation and decorum and his distrust of the personal and the passionate—in all this (and more) the Christian Greeks of Constantinople found a philosophical basis for their faith in an order of things that, in its divinely ordained stasis and its dependence upon authoritarian abstractions, had far more in common with Egyptian thought than with that of the Biblical prophets, of Jesus and his apostles, or of Lucretius and Seneca. The Byzantine Christian was fascinated with metaphysical conceptions of being, above all with Christological questions concerning the nature of trinitarian Deity; but he quite lost touch with what Harvey Cox has aptly called the "gritty historicity" of Biblical (and of earlier Roman) thought.

While there is some disagreement among scholars as to the nether limit of the Byzantine era in the history of art, it is generally conceded that its first flowering occurred in the reign of Justinian (527-565). Though most of the manuscript and mosaic art that was produced at that time in the eastern centers of the empire has been destroyed, there survive from Justinian's day two major monuments that we must consider with some care: the Church of the Holy Wisdom (Hagia Sophia) in Constantinople, and the Church of San Vitale, together with its mosaics, in Ravenna. Both buildings are domed, central churches—a type we have not thus far examined.

The central church appears on the scene in the fourth century at about the same time as the basilican building and has an ancestry that goes back well before that time. Whereas the basilica is associated with the forum, the law courts, and the aristocratic house, the central form was commonly used as a mausoleum (as in the church of Sta. Costanza in Rome, which was originally built to house the sarcophagi of Constantine's daughters), as a chapel over the grave of a Christian martyr, and as a baptistry (wherein one "died" insofar as his worldly life was concerned and entered into a new life as a member of the saintly community of the saved.) The basilica is essentially a *city* building; its rectangular patterns are akin to those of the great majority of urban structures and to the Roman conception of the city itself. The central church, on the other hand, turns inward upon itself and is typically related to experiences that transcend our earthly existence. It is organized around the vertical axis that connects the floor plane with the apex of the dome overhead, while the basilica is governed by the axis that extends horizontally from the entrance toward the altar in the apse. Throughout the Middle Ages the basilican form embodied the characteristic concerns, or expressed the socio-political orientation, of the western or Roman Catholic branch of the church, while the central structure was associated with the religious attitudes that were predominant in the eastern or Greek Orthodox branch. The long rectangular basilica is rarely encountered in the East after the fifth century.

This is not to say, however, that the central church is otherworldly and without political implications. On the contrary, it is closely related to the theory of the state that was propagated by Justinian and his followers, according to which all power descends through celestial and terrestrial hierarchies from God, whose vicar on earth the emperor is. Both the imperial office and the structure of the state were sacred. Indeed, the "sacralization" of the state that was not only countenanced but promoted by the Byzantine church far exceeded anything the Roman Empire would have claimed for itself in the days when Christians were suffering martyrdom for rejecting its halfhearted pretensions to being of divine ordination.

It has been fashionable for some time to describe the Byzantine conception of rulership as "caesaropapist." The word implies that the emperor was both caesar and pope, undisputed head of state and church alike. It is generally agreed today, however, that his authority was usually more limited than that. Certainly an emperor could influence the election of the patriarch of Constantinople and could sometimes have removed from office a patriarch who opposed him; but the patriarch was not the subservient lackey of the emperor. Perhaps the only legitimate application of the term *caesaropapist* is to the reign of Justinian himself, for he undoubtedly aspired to being a priest-king. It is upon his conception of kingship that the Ravenna mosaics and the Church of Hagia Sophia would seem to bear.

Hagia Sophia was begun in February, 532, less than six weeks after a hundred-year-old church on the site had been destroyed in the course of the Nika Sedition—a ten-day period of rioting by the disfranchised and frustrated populace who tried, briefly and disastrously, to regain their right to *do* something as responsible Roman citizens rather than simply to submit to an absolute despotism. At the height of the disorder the rebellious citizenry gathered in the Hippodrome, alongside the Sacred Palace, and declared a man of their own choosing to be em-

peror. After vacillating and contemplating flight, Justinian was persuaded by his wife to stand firm, to call up military reinforcements and,
according to the historian Procopius, to have thirty thousand of his
Christian citizens slaughtered in the stadium. He then had his architect
Anthemius of Tralles (assisted by one Isidorus of Miletus) rush to
completion his plans for a splendid new church to replace the old one.
Despite its great size, the building was completed in less than six years;
according to an anonymous writer of the time, it was built by ten thousand workmen, and at a cost approaching $100,000,000 in present-day
terms.

The church (Fig. 9) is commonly described as a domed basilica,
but no such categorization does justice to so unique an invention. Anthemius began with a plan that, as Emerson Swift has pointed out, is
similar in both its shape and its actual measurements to that of the
Basilica of Maxentius in Rome. That this was in fact the source of the
architect's scheme cannot, of course, be demonstrated. What matters is

Figure 9. Interior, Hagia Sophia, Constantinople (Istanbul), 532-537.
(Courtesy of Dr. Franz Stoedtner, Düsseldorf.)

I · T - Turkey

that he rejected the kind of columniated basilica that had appealed to Constantine and his successors and revived instead the tradition of imperial grandiosity that had lapsed after the building of the Basilica of Maxentius and the Baths of Constantine. Anthemius found his inspiration partly, it would appear, in the imperial buildings of Rome and partly in the domed churches that were especially numerous in Asia Minor and Syria. He must have known that his patron had no interest in a form that smacked of republican equalitarianism; that phase of state-church relationship was now at an end.

Yet his work is no mere pastiche of secondhand ideas. It is one of the boldest inventions of the medieval world, affirming there to be a new relationship between the civil and the divine. In the wake of the Nika uprising the Emperor evidently intended to make it clear once

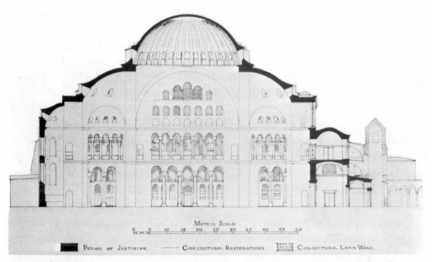

Figure 10. Section, Hagia Sophia, Constantinople. (Reproduced with permission from: Swift, E., *Hagia Sophia*. New York, Columbia University Press, 1940, p. 214.)

and for all that his power was from above—an emanation of the Divine Wisdom that would brook no challenge from the lower orders. Externally as well as internally Hagia Sophia is dominated by its enormous dome, 108 feet in diameter and rising to a height of 182 feet above the floor (Fig. 10). It is the one simple, complete shape toward which all the lesser and partial shapes are drawn and from which they descend; it hovers overhead as if floating on a ring of light, or, as Procopius expressed it, "as if let down from heaven on a golden chain." In the center of the dome there probably was at one time (and may well still be, beneath the Arabic inscriptions that now cover the area) a bust-length image of the Pantocrator, or of Christ the Almighty, looking directly down upon the congregation below. Such an image is to be found in the central dome of many a later Byzantine church, (e.g., Daphni), making it plain that the architectural form was meant to be associated in men's minds with the authority of a supreme Ruler.

There are 104 columns in Justinian's church, all told; but many of these are not visible from the main floor, nor is there the slightest suggestion that the columns have any part in supporting the dome. The cupola is actually carried, by means of pendentives, on four huge arches, which in turn spring from four great masonry piers. However, the latter are screened from view by colonnades and diaphragm walls, so that one is scarcely aware of the structural apparatus that bears the dome's weight. Procopius was perfectly right: the dome appears to be a hovering golden concavity that does not need to be borne up from below. In the basilican church, as in all earlier hypostyle halls, the principal architectural feature is the floor plane—the place of assembly where many members gather as a community and where many columns stand together in order to support the sheltering superstructure of the building. This was the symbolism Justinian and Anthemius rejected. Little wonder that the column plays a minor role at best in later Byzantine architecture, and is often absent altogether (cf. Daphni and the early Russian churches of the twelfth century). In all such buildings one is moved, not by the collaboration of working members in a lucid system of construction, as had so often been the case in earlier architecture, but by the vast concavities of the interior, by the extravagant abundance of gold and of colored marbles, and above all, by the mystery of light, which is a present and felt reality in the church.

In a lunette over the main doorway into Hagia Sophia there was later installed a mosaic (Fig. 11) that further explicates the meaning of the building. In the center of the area, against a gold ground, we see an implacably frontal Christ, seated upon his celestial throne. At his feet the Emperor Leo VI prostrates himself, in utter submission to the divine Source of his authority. The great church is, in effect, Christ's resplendent palace. Yet its import will be missed if it is not kept in mind that Hagia Sophia adjoined the Sacred Palace of the Byzantine emperors, within which, there is reason to believe, the imperial throne room was also a domed central building, smaller than, but generically similar to, Hagia Sophia itself. There the emperor sat on *his* throne, before which dignitaries prostrated *themselves,* in keeping

Figure 11. *Leo VI before the Throne of Christ.* Lunette mosaic, Hagia Sophia, *ca.* 900. (Courtesy of Skira International, Inc., New York.)

with an elaborate system of court ceremony, the exhausting ramifications of which were recorded in the eleventh century by the Emperor Constantine Porphyrogenitus. And we may suppose that when the governors of the various provinces, who received their authority from the emperor, sat on *their* thrones, humbler persons prostrated themselves or otherwise made obeisance before them—and so on down the line. Hagia Sophia was, for all time, *the* imperial church, to which all other churches in the empire were subsidiary, even as all other officials were subservient to the emperor. No building of comparable size was ever thereafter erected in any Byzantine city; for to have built another such church would have been to challenge the sacred structure of the empire itself.

It is partly for this reason that later Byzantine churches are small, even minute, by comparison with the great monastic and cathedral churches of the twelfth and thirteenth centuries in the West. They make no boast of the proud superiority of a local organization, or of the independence of a free and self-governing city. Even the larger cities of the Byzantine world characteristically possessed several small neighborhood churches but no large one that could dominate the center of the city as its cathedral dominates the town of Chartres. Moreover, it was in the nature of the Eastern autocracy that it had to discourage the tradition of popular assembly that had caused the Pnyx in Athens and the Rostrum in Rome to become fundamental symbols of the body politic. In the Greek church the role of preaching, or of haranguing the people on moral issues from a rostrum-like pulpit, was of little importance; indeed, it soon became customary to erect an *iconostasis*, or decorated screen, between the congregation and the altar, thereby minimizing the direct participation of the laity in the sacred mysteries that were celebrated in the apse.

It was perhaps unfortunate for the later history of Europe that the Byzantine church should have carried Christianity to Russia, in the late tenth century, for she could not take with her the tradition of civic assembly that is essential to our conception of political life in the West. That Graeco-Roman tradition was kept alive by the Roman church throughout the Dark Age, but it was not transmitted to the Russian steppe. The cathedral church of Moscow, the Church of the Assumption, was inside the Kremlin, where it bore no relationship and little resemblance to the Roman public halls from which the medieval basilica was sprung. Nor does Ivan the Terrible's gaudy Church of St. Basil the Blessed on Red Square perform a function comparable to that of the western cathedrals. Contrary to appearances, it is not a large church at all but only a collection of nine small chapels, even the largest of which provides very little room for a congregation of worshipers.

But let us return to Justinian and consider our second monument from his reign, the Church of San Vitale in Ravenna (Fig. 12). The building was begun, it seems, by Bishop Ecclesius in 526, the year of the death of Theodoric the Great. Since that Arian Ostrogoth left no strong successor, the Orthodox forces undertook at once to regain supremacy in the city. The church was begun in the year preceding Justinian's accession to the throne, but it should be kept in mind that he had served as co-emperor with his uncle, Justin I, for several years before the latter's death in 527. What with the generic resemblance between San Vitale and the Church of SS. Sergius and Bacchus in Constantinople, which was also under construction in the 520s (we cannot fix its dates exactly), there is good reason to suppose that the patronage and power of the eastern capital were behind San Vitale from the beginning—that it was designed specifically to be an imperial church. (Efforts have been made at tracing its genealogical descent from various earlier buildings, both eastern and western, but it is important to remember always that buildings are not biological organisms. They do not marry one another and beget children; they are the inventions of architectural artists who are emotionally involved with, and concerned to address, a human and institutional situation. What other buildings a given architect may have known, and what specific ideas

Figure 12. Interior, looking toward apse, San Vitale, Ravenna, ca. 526-45. (Courtesy of Hirmer Fotoarchiv München.)

he may have derived from them, can never be determined, whether he be ancient, medieval, or modern.)

Ravenna was brought under the political control of Constantinople in the late 530s, when the city was captured by Belisarius. The apsidal mosaics of San Vitale were installed in the following decade. They declare the presence in the city of the sacred authority of the Emperor, even though Justinian may never have visited Ravenna at all. The mosaics that survive (those of the central dome have been lost) are located in the choir of the church, where the altar stands, and in the apse, which probably contained the throne of the archbishop. The choir mosaics deal with episodes from the life of Moses, a leader and lawgiver to whom Justinian wanted to be likened, and with four themes of offering taken from the Book of Genesis, all of which bear upon the significance of the Eucharist.

The principal mosaics, however, are the three that are in the apse. In the half dome that covers the area we see Christ seated on the sphere of the universe (Fig. 13). He is flanked by two angels and two

Figure 13. Apsidal mosaic, San Vitale, Ravenna, ca. 545. (Courtesy of Dr. Franz Stoedtner, Düsseldorf.)

3

saints, all of whom stand in a paradisiacal garden and against a gold ground. Christ is dressed in purple trimmed with gold, the angels in white trimmed with purple. The angel to Christ's right introduces St. Vitalis, an early martyr to whom the church is dedicated, who extends covered hands to receive the crown of victory which Christ holds out to him. The other angel introduces Bishop Ecclesius, who had died before the building was finished; he is dressed mainly in purple and, with covered hands, presents to Christ an image of San Vitale itself. Plainly there exists in heaven a hierarchy, the gradations of which are indicated by position (seated over standing, central over lateral, right over left), by cut and color of costume, by types of halo, by degree of frontality, and so on. Here are the archetypes of the patterns that so rigorously governed the institutional life of medieval Byzantium.

Under the two sides of this image, on the side walls of the apse, are two celebrated mosaics in rectangular frames (worldly shapes, in contrast to the celestial sphericity of the image above) in which we see Justinian and his court on the left (*i.e.*, on Christ's right) and the Empress Theodora and her court on the opposite wall. The figures are presented as in a procession; both the Emperor and the Empress are bringing offerings to Christ. The processional movement is obvious in Theodora's mosaic, but it is subtly disguised in Justinian's (Fig. 14); for though the Emperor holds out his offering toward Christ, who is to his left, he is represented frontally and in the exact center of his mosaic panel, even as is Christ in the dome mosaic. He is dressed mostly in purple and gold (only his right sleeve is white); his earthly position is analogous to Christ's in heaven. And yet Justinian is not centered among his attendants: there are eight persons on his right and only four on his left. In other words, the three priests on the right occupy as much space as do seven secular figures on the left—with the result that Justinian is kept within the context of the secular group that becomes progressively more crowded as its figures are farther removed from the enthroned Christ. Moreover, the clerics are directly below the left portion of the dome mosaic, the frame of which, if extended downward, would cut through the figure of Justinian. All told, there are thirteen persons represented in the mosaic, corresponding to the number of Christ and his disciples. But which is the Christ figure, Justinian or Archbishop Maximianus?

Many things would appear to suggest a competitive relationship between the two. Maximianus and his fellow clerics are drawn to a larger scale than the other figures. Since the archbishop's feet extend to a lower level than Justinian's, he seems both taller and more advanced than the Emperor, and certainly he is closer to Christ. Maxi-

Figure 14. *Justinian and his Court.* San Vitale, Ravenna, ca. 545.
(Courtesy of Dr. Franz Stoedtner, Düsseldorf.)

mianus is in exactly the same pose as the Emperor (left hand covered,
right hand holding an object at waist level), but whereas the Emperor
carries an offering, the Archbishop carries a symbol of authority (a
jeweled cross). His facial expression is personal and intense, making
him more vividly present to the observer than is Justinian, who is a bit
overwhelmed by his emblems and badges. Needless to say, the artist
was able to see Maximianus regularly, but he may never have seen
Justinian at all. Then, too, it was probably Maximianus who decided
that his predecessor, Bishop Ecclesius, should be shown wearing in
paradise as much purple as Justinian wears on earth. And finally, Maximianus has his name over his head. Although it would have been un-
seemly to identify the Emperor by name, the presence of the word
MAXIMIANUS provides an accent in the composition that competes
with, and partially offsets, the central emphasis that is determined by
Justinian's jeweled crown and honorific halo.

We have no reason to suppose that there was personal rivalry or
animosity between the two men. A much larger problem is involved:

that of the interrelationship of the two imperial institutions of the Middle Ages, the empire and the church. Each conceived itself to be in some ultimate sense all-powerful. The autocratic emperor was the final source of all authority in the state and had the power of life and death over all its citizens. The head of the church, on the other hand, held the power to excommunicate—to eject any man from the community of the faithful and to cut him off from all hope of salvation—and he could wield this power against the emperor himself if need be. It followed, of course, that the relation of church and state was an inherently precarious one, especially in the West, where the popes were inclined to regard themselves as the lawful heirs to the throne of Constantine. (It may be of some importance that the mosaics under discussion are in Italy rather than in Constantinople, and in a city where the archbishop in question was a powerful civil as well as ecclesiastical administrator.)

Toward the end of the eleventh century Pope Gregory VII assumed, in effect, the position of an emperor, going so far as to wear imperial dress and a kingly crown and to compel the secular ruler to humble himself before him. Justinian, on the other hand, virtually assumed the role of priest. There are excellent grounds for believing, with Otto von Simson, that what the Emperor and Empress are carrying in their respective vessels in the San Vitale mosaics are the bread and wine of the Eucharist; which they bring directly to God's throne—even as Abraham and his wife Sarah are shown to serve the three angels (representing the Trinity) in the left-hand choir mosaic, or as the priest-king Melchisedek offers bread and wine at an altar in the right-hand mosaic. Looking at the matter from Justinian's point of view, we can attach another significance to the purple vestments of Bishop Ecclesius in the dome mosaic; for not only is the priest similar to the emperor (as it may have seemed to Maximianus), but it is equally true that the emperor is like the priest. This is not to strain the evidence beyond all reason; it is of just such intellectual subtleties that the fabric of Byzantine thought was typically woven.

We do not have space in which to consider the later history of mosaic art in the East. The history is a long one, with periods of dormancy and others of vitality; but whether dormant or renascent it offers little that is of interest to us, for Byzantine art underwent surprisingly little change or development in subsequent centuries. In some respects the Ravenna mosaics are livelier and more interesting than any of the later ones. The tendency of the style was toward a crystallization of certain formulas for the rendering of faces, drapery, gestures, cities, and rudimentary landscape features. As had been the case in

Egypt, where certain formulas were kept in use for as long as three thousand years, the Byzantine abhorrence of change was bound up with the innate conservatism of an absolute monarchy that cloaked itself in an aura of divinity. Only the things of the world undergo change; what is divine is eternal.

But whereas Egyptian art never advanced beyond the conventions of an archaic style, that of Byzantium was developed in a cultivated urban world that was thoroughly conversant with Graeco-Roman art and thought. We encounter the curious and rather modern phenomenon, therefore, of a reductive and archaistic art that was provided by its patrons with a highly sophisticated philosophical justification (though one that is wholly inapplicable to modern art). According to Byzantine theory,[1] which was essentially Platonic, the image is related to its prototype somewhat as a mirrored reflection is related to a real object, or as a shadow is related to whatever "casts" it. Imperfect though its reflection may be (ancient and medieval mirrors were grossly inferior to the ones we use today), the image has a direct and self-validating relationship to a sacred subject whose importance greatly transcends that of the artist, of the work of art, and of the observer and his act of experiencing it. Its significance derives from its prototype and not at all from the inventive originality of the man who made it; wherefore the creative genius of the artist was as little celebrated in Constantinople as it had been in Memphis and Thebes.

Plainly the theory would have militated against the introduction of novel departures and would have tended to endow traditional forms with a kind of sacred authenticity. Indeed, it encouraged something so close to out-and-out idolatry as to cause the Emperor Leo the Isaurian to attempt to abolish images from the churches altogether. Leo met with immediate and vociferous opposition, especially from two large classes of the population, monks and women. During most of the period from 726 until 843 the Iconoclasts, or image-breakers, prevailed in court circles; but the icons were restored under the infamous Irene in the 790s and again by Theodora in 843, whereafter a truce was reached, and Byzantine art entered upon a new era of productivity. One effect of the prolonged struggle, however, was to bring about the imposition of even stricter conventions within which the artist had to work.

Inside the shadowy confines of the domed Orthodox church, whose reverberating concavities the mosaicist was wont to people with a host of grave, quiescent figures, the iconic art of Byzantium was no doubt superbly effective. It helped to set the church apart from earthly things and to introduce its members to a world of eternal serenity. But when, in the eleventh and twelfth centuries, the style was exported from Constantinople to Sicily and to Venice, it became agitated and anecdotal, touched with something of the turmoil of Romanesque art. To speak of the *Nativity* mosaic from the Palatine Chapel in Palermo as being Byzantine is to stretch the term considerably; for this is an art that, in its concern for busy detail and for a variety of activities and relationships, looks forward already to the Renaissance. But these are matters we shall have to deal with in a later chapter.

FOOTNOTES

[1]See Demus, Otto, *Byzantine Mosaic Decoration.* Boston: Boston Book & Art Shop, Inc., 1951.

3

Clovis

The Dark Age

In the last years of the fourth century and throughout the fifth, western Europe was overrun by wave after wave of migrant barbarians —Goths, Huns, Vandals, Alemans, Franks, Burgundians, Jutes, Saxons, Thuringians, Salians, and others. Even Rome could not, or would not, defend itself against them. By the end of the fifth century Britain, Gaul, Spain, North Africa, and most of Italy were in the hands of barbarian chieftains. North Africa and Italy were reconquered for Constantinople by Belisarius in the 530s, but they were lost to the Lombards and to the Saracens in the seventh century.

In 481, in the Belgian town of Tournai, a fifteen-year-old boy named Chlodwig (Clovis) was made king of a local Frankish tribe. With cunning, cruelty, and boundless ambition, the boy proceeded to bring under his control the Germanic lands not only of northern Gaul and the Rhineland but eventually of southern Gaul as well, which he seized from the Visigoths around 507. He was persuaded by a Burgundian queen to embrace the faith of the Roman church (most of the barbarians inclined toward Arianism) and was baptized at Rheims shortly before the year 500. Yet it was typical of the religious attitudes of that day—so different from those of the time of Constantine, when no one joined the church until he was ready to lead a new life—that though the young king's conversion was hailed as a major triumph for the church, it made not the slightest difference in his personal conduct or in that of his Christian descendants, most of whom were as murderous and rapacious as had been their pagan forebears. Nor did the church feel obliged to censure their conduct. It was not to the artist alone that men's actions in the world had ceased to be significant; a "new morality" had established itself throughout the society.

Clovis founded a Frankish dynasty that is called Merovingian, but he did not establish a government in any sense of the word that we would accept today. As Ferdinand Lot puts it, civil administration for the Merovingians meant only "exploitation of the State by the King," who looked upon the kingdom as a private property that existed solely for his own satisfaction. It never occurred to the Merovingian ruler that he had any obligation toward, any responsibility for the welfare of, the people over whom he ruled. Like all his successors, Clovis had no fixed capital city. He headed a peripatetic court that moved about among the principal towns of his domain. His kingdom was ruled by migratory persons rather than by established institutions; wherefore it had no need for the art of architecture. The few buildings that survive from Merovingian Europe are but vestigial remnants of the meaningful architecture of the Roman Empire. With the decline of building there disappeared also the related arts of mosaic and of sculpture—for which there would have been no demand, even if the impoverished Franks could have afforded them. As had been the case during the dark age that followed the fall of Minoan-Mycenaean civilization around 1100 B.C., the typical art objects of the Merovingian period were small, portable things, such as brooches, buckles, crosses, and manuscripts—and very few of these have been preserved.

This brings us to the matter of the illustrated or decorated book— a subject that was not taken up earlier, partly because it raises certain special problems of its own that need to be dealt with separately, and partly because, in the urban societies of late Roman and Byzantine times, it was a minor art, inferior to architecture and to the making of larger images for public display, even as has been the case in the modern world for the past 550 years. Moreover, the earlier phases of the history of book illustration are of little interest for the simple reason that no examples have come down to us from Graeco-Roman antiquity, and only a tiny handful from the fourth, fifth, and sixth centuries.

What relation does a picture have to a written text? What does it mean for one to *illustrate* a book? So far as we can tell, the Romans would have answered such questions much as we would today. The earliest illustrated manuscript we possess from the Roman world is a copy of Virgil's *Aeneid* in the Vatican Library in Rome. Although it is believed to date from the late fourth century, it probably preserves a tradition of book illustration that goes back to the days of the Republic, just as the basic conventions of illustration in the twentieth century are similar to those of the early Renaissance. The text is written in large, evenly spaced capital letters that are meant to be as legible as Virgil's text is lucid. The manuscript contains a great many illustrations (originally some 250) that are set into the text at appropriate points within neatly painted rectangular frames (Fig. 15). Though the pictures are

Figure 15. *Harbor Scene.* Vatican Virgil (Vat. lat. 3525), *ca.* 375.
(By permission of Biblioteca Apostolica Vaticana.) R-8

small and rather clumsy in style, they plainly preserve a conception
of illustration that takes us back to Pompeian wall paintings of the
time of Nero and Vespasian. Deeds are acted out within architectural
interiors and against open and architectural landscapes in which the
various perspective devices of orthogonal convergence, diminution, and
atmospheric gradation are frequently employed. The artist took it for
granted that it was his function to assist the reader in an imaginative
recreation or visualization of the dramatic action the author describes.
As does Virgil, he invites the reader to identify himself with the characters in the epic and to experience with them their various adventures.

Neither the poet nor the painter seems ever to have questioned the axiomatic assumption that what matters in human being is a man's emotional involvement in consequential events that occur in space and time, or that value resides ultimately in his morally responsible and spiritually responsive relationship to other persons, singly and in groups, as he encounters them in the historical world. The fundamental metaphor in terms of which the artist comprehends his existence is that of the drama: the world is a stage, man is an actor who must make decisions and pursue goals, and there is a *play*—that is, the kind of overarching destiny to which Virgil refers in the opening lines of the *Aeneid*, where he sings of Aeneas as a man "driven by fate" to the Lavinian shores, there to play a decisive part in the founding of Rome.

By chance, there has come down to us another manuscript of the works of Virgil that was probably made less than a hundred years after the one we have just considered. This book (the "Roman Virgil") contains very few illustrations; the artist was far less interested in a visual savoring of the varied action of the *Aeneid*. Though the pictures are still framed, they reveal a strong tendency toward the kind of schematic flattening observed in *The Parting of Abraham and Lot* in Sta. Maria Maggiore. In rendering a battle scene, for instance, the artist places five or six large figures in the left half of his rectangle, a similar number in the right half, and leaves a narrow blank area down the center. There is no horizontal ground plane, no perspective diminution, no rendering of effects of light or atmosphere. The scene is about as lively as a processional mosaic from San Vitale. Or if he pictures Dido and Aeneas dining together (Fig. 16), he eliminates the temporal dimension of their existence by forcing the scene into a pattern that is so symmetrical, so emblematic, that it admits the possibility of only one kind of movement—that of a liturgical ceremony. All that pertains to decision-making, to the dramatic interaction of different persons pursuing different purposes, and to the problematical outcome of such interaction, is wholly suppressed.

Equally interesting is the illustration (Fig. 17) that accompanies the *Georgics*, Virgil's poetic treatise on rural husbandry, which had been written in the first century B.C., at a time when luminous pastoral landscapes were much in favor among cultivated Romans. In those earlier paintings one sees a spatial continuum that extends outward from the observer and into a pictured scene that recedes toward the horizon. In affirming the continuity of the spatial world, the artist declared also his faith in the wholeness and continuity of the observer's own self: for such paintings (whether Roman or Renaissance) reveal to us an order of things that is bound together by an act of comprehension on

Figure 16. *Dido and Aeneas.* Roman Virgil (Vat. lat. 3867), *ca.* 450.
(Courtesy of Dr. Franz Stoedtner, Düsseldorf.)   R~18 9

the part of a man who knows himself to occupy a central and responsible position in that order, which is the world. What we see in the
Codex Romanus, on the other hand, is no landscape at all, even though
it contains many of the ingredients of such a scene. The artist has
destroyed the continuum of the world and, along with it, the dramatic
and personal involvement of the observer with the image. One might
say that he has "decomposed" the world, has broken it apart into a
scatter pattern which invites no emotional response from the observer
and which in its very nature denies the possibility of significant narrative action in space and time.

Carl Nordenfalk attributes this development to "provincialism"—
that is, to ignorance or backwardness on the part of the artist, whom
he assumes to be a bumpkin from some outlying district. In this he
is quite mistaken, I believe; for he overlooks the fact that a similar
development has taken place in modern art during the past hundred
years, and that that development has emanated entirely from a few big
cities and has been resisted tooth and nail in the "provinces." The
change occurred rather suddenly in the 1860s, since when our leading
modern artists have totally abandoned the illustration of narrative action, have been less and less concerned with rendering a stage-like
spatial continuum, have rejected all chiaroscuro, and have shown great

Figure 17. *Pastoral Scene.* Roman Virgil (Vat. lat. 3867), *ca.* 450.
(By permission of Biblioteca Apostolica Vaticana.)

fondness for scatter patterns (whether in the street scenes of the Impressionists or in the random juxtapositions so characteristic of Klee and Miro).

Yet one may argue that only what is dead readily decomposes. For reasons that are obscure to us, even though we are ourselves living through a similar course of development, a significant number of persons in the late Roman world (whether their number was large or small matters less, perhaps, than does their position in the social and political order) lost confidence in the old metaphors, the old unspoken presuppositions that had made it possible for the Romans to think of themselves as being men of the kind one sees in the typical Roman portrait of the late Republic or of the early Empire. The dimension of "character" disappeared from ancient portraiture in the fourth century; in modern art it disappeared with Cézanne.

The abandonment of those metaphors had two obvious consequences in early medieval book illustration. In the first place, there was a rapid decline of interest in the illustration of the storied events set forth in written texts. Narrative imagery gave way to other kinds of visual invention, much as the narrative painting of Ingres and Delacroix (both of whom died in the 1860s) has been supplanted by a nonillustrational and largely nonfigural art in the mid twentieth century. And secondly, where narrative illustration did survive, it was dealt with in such a way as not to involve the imaginative participation of the reader-observer in the deeds or the emotions of the characters represented. Let us briefly consider two examples of what we suppose to be sixth-century manuscript painting (their date is disputed), one believed to be from the East, the other from the West.

The first of these is the *Vienna Genesis*—a fragmentary copy of the Book of Genesis, the Greek text of which is inscribed in silver letters on purple-stained vellum. (The same means are employed in two closely related manuscripts, the *Codex Rossanensis* in Rossano, Italy, and the *Sinope* fragment in Paris.) The illustrations are now unframed; the figures lie on the surface of the page much as the letters do. The little scenes (which are yet not *skenai*, since there is hardly a suggestion of a stage plane or stage space) sometimes involve several episodes that are strung out sequentially as are the verses in the text, without regard for considerations of temporal or spatial unity. For the page on which the story of Joseph and Potiphar's wife is recounted (Gen. 39 : 7-20), the artist depicted Joseph's freeing himself from the woman's clutches—and then, for want of anything else to portray, he filled the greater part of his space with a miscellany of irrelevant

Figure 18. *Joseph and Potiphar's Wife.* Vienna Genesis (National Library, Vienna), *ca.* 525. (Illustration from: W. von Hartel & F. Wickhoff, *Die Wiener Genesis.* Vienna: F. Tempsky, 1895.)

household scenes and finally with a pair of little trees. Building, figures, and trees all rest on straight ground lines.

It is hard for us to imagine in what frame of mind, or for what spiritual or psychological purposes, people read the Bible in the sixth century, for the illustrations do nothing to illuminate one's understanding, or to intensify one's imaginative recreation, of the narrative account. They do serve, however, to make the book itself an object of great beauty. The colors are clear and fresh, the images attractive to the eye, the purple and silver sumptuous to behold.

The second example, again a fragment of an initially larger work, is known as the Ashburnham Pentateuch. No one knows where or when it was made; possibly in Spain or North Africa in the late sixth or seventh century. Its nineteen full-page illustrations are inside red-lined rectangular frames, but the function of the frame is now still further removed from that of the "window" frame of antiquity. Within a single rectangle the artist may dispose as many as eight or ten little clusters of figures, animals, and buildings, each related to a different passage in the Biblical text. One frame may contain both indoor and outdoor happenings. What chiefly separates one episode from another is the color of the background in a given area on the page. Oftentimes, as in the page illustrating the story of Jacob and Esau (Fig. 19), one would have to know the story very well indeed, or would have to read the text carefully, verse by verse, in order to know what the figures are doing. (It should be kept in mind as a general principle that, no

Figure 19. *Story of Jacob and Esau.* Ashburnham Pentateuch. (Bib. nat., nouv. acq. lat. 2334), *ca.* 600? (Courtesy of Bibliothèque nationale, Paris.)

F-1

matter what medieval churchmen may have said to the contrary, pictures cannot *tell* stories. The purpose of illustrating a book, or of decorating the walls or windows of a church with narrative imagery, is never an instructional one.) What is fascinating about the Ashburnham pictures is the liveliness of the artist's invention. His rhythms are now stark, now undulating, now clattering, as he substitutes a new kind of artistic vitality for the dramatic emotionality that seemed no longer meaningful to him. (Again many modern parallels will come to mind.) Where this sprightly innovation might have led we do not know, for to the best of our meager knowledge, the work had no immediate successors. The conquest of North Africa and of Spain by the Moors in the seventh and eighth centuries probably brought to an end the activity of the scriptorium that produced the manuscript.

II

At about the time that this development was snuffed out there began another one, in the British Isles, that was destined to accomplish great things before it, too, was extinguished around the year 800. Christianity had been carried to Britain by the Romans, of course; but in the fourth century the Roman legions were gradually withdrawn, and eventually Roman Britain was cut off from its Mediterranean base by the Germanic conquest of Gaul. In the fifth century the island was itself invaded by Germans (Angles, Saxons, Jutes) who displaced the Romanized Britons, pushing them westward toward Cornwall and Wales, where they were gradually assimilated into a predominantly Celtic population. In 432 the Roman faith had been carried to Ireland by a Briton, St. Patrick, whose Christian successors were apparently in touch with the Celtic church in Wales. Contact with Rome was reestablished in 597, when Pope Gregory the Great sent a missionary named Augustine to convert the pagan Saxons. St. Augustine established himself at Canterbury, where he met with such success that he was made a bishop and was eventually put in charge of all the churches of England, thereby becoming the first Archbishop of Canterbury. Under conditions of relative stability that prevailed in the seventh and eighth centuries, the now-united Anglo-Celtic monastic church, with its spiritual and administrative center on the island of Iona, became the most active in all Europe, sending out its missionaries to found churches and monasteries not only in the British Isles but up and down the Continent.

Every new church they established needed at least a small number of books, to be used in the services at the altar, so that the Anglo-Celtic scriptoria were kept busy turning out manuscripts for liturgical use. It is important to remember that the books were not made to be read for pleasure or instruction; in a country where illiteracy was nearly universal, the act of reading came to be associated, even in the minds of the monks themselves, with the mysteries that were celebrated in the church rather than with any of the secular activities to which we relate reading and writing today. This is not to say that the monks shunned or despised the world. We know little about them; but obviously it would be a mistake for anyone to conclude from the "abstract" nature of modern art that ours is an especially "unworldly" age. The issues are not so simple as that. All we can say is that the Celtic artist did not find the wellsprings of his art to arise out of his experience of, or experiences within, the visible world around him.

His manuscript style was so different from anything that had previously been produced in the Christian West that one is tempted to join Nordenfalk in calling it the "last flowering of prehistoric art." It is almost exclusively an art of decorative patternization, and the patterns employed are mostly derived from the barbarian art that had been brought into England by the Germanic invaders. Its vocabulary consisted of strap-work patterns, interlaced reptilian forms, geometrical figures, and ingenious devices woven out of letters. Except for the letters, these are the forms that had long been used by Germanic craftsmen for the embellishment of sword handles, brooches, shields, ships' prows, and the like. It would appear that the pagan art of the folk-wandering age had been taken over, lock, stock, and barrel, by these new-made Christians, the genuineness of whose conversion one might even find reason to doubt.

Yet these manuscripts were not produced by barbarians. We know beyond a doubt that the Celtic monks had access to illustrated books that had been imported from Italy, and that not only Latin but also Greek texts were still being read in Britain, at a time when Greek was no longer known in most of the West. At least one Anglo-Celtic divine, Alcuin of York, was esteemed by Charlemagne as one of the most cultivated and learned members of his court at Aachen. Far from being isolated provincials, rooted still in "prehistoric" ways, the British clergy at this point were apparently among the best-educated and best-traveled men in Christendom, in touch with Rome and with centers of learning throughout western Europe, perhaps even with Coptic Egypt. Their repudiation of narrative and figural imagery was part of a much more general development that had been taking shape since before the fall of Rome.

Let us consider but a single page (Fig. 20) from what was in all likelihood the terminal masterpiece of the Anglo-Celtic style, the Book of Kells—a copy of the Gospels that was probably made at St. Columba's monastery on Iona just before its destruction by the "Danes" around 802. At that time the book was presumably taken to Ireland, where a new Columban monastery was established at Kells. After the dissolution of the monasteries by Henry VIII the book eventually found its way into the library of Trinity College in Dublin. Though the manuscript is for the most part written in an unusually well-formed and legible script, each of the four Gospels is introduced with a page on which the first words of the text are woven into a fabric which, for sheer intricacy of

Ireland

Figure 20. First page of the Gospel of Mark, the Book of Kells, ca. 800. (By permission of the Board of Trinity College, Dublin.)

conception and virtuosity of execution, has never been surpassed in western art. With patient study one can discover, in the page here illustrated, the opening words of the Gospel of Mark: "Initium evangelii Jesu Christi" ("The beginning of the gospel of Jesus Christ"). The words are "legible," of course, only to someone who already knows them; but it needs be remembered that, as has been mentioned, one must already know a story in order to "read" a narrative illustration. When one looks at a representation of the conversion of Paul, say, or of the resurrection of Lazarus, one has to relate what one already knows to a set of visual symbols, and one takes satisfaction in discovering how the visible shapes and colors bear upon that prior knowledge. The monks who read from the Book of Kells must have found a similar pleasure in discovering the familiar Latin words among the myriad patterns within which they are embedded. The experience was a highly inbred one, however, both for the painter and for the reader. The artist found delight, not in his imaginative involvement with the content of the Gospel but in his own fecund inventiveness—in his ability to take the simple materials and tools of a scribe and to bring forth a marvelous profusion of shapes which, though they are without expressive value, beguile the eye and the mind with their formal qualities. For the reader, such illuminations enhanced the pleasure and excitement of handling and of looking at the book and of deciphering the letters in the act of reading, as well as lending an aura of mystery, even of magic, to that act.2

III

In the middle of the eighth century, when the vitality of the Anglo-Celtic church was at its height, there came to the Frankish throne a new dynasty of kings. In 751 the last of the now ineffectual Merovingian rulers was ousted by his Mayor of the Palace, Pepin the Short; and in 754 Pope Stephen II journeyed north to lend his sanction to Pepin's usurpation by annointing him king at St. Denis, near Paris—in return for which favor he solicited the king's aid against the Lombards, who had by now seized the greater part of the Italian peninsula. Pepin promised assistance and invaded Italy twice in the 750s; but while he won victories, he did not conquer the Lombard kingdom. He was succeeded, in 768, by his son Charles (later known as Charles the Great, or Charlemagne), a young man of immense energy and ambition, who led his Frankish army across the Alps in the early 770s, defeated the Lombard king Desiderius at Pavia in the summer of 774, and went on to Rome, where he was received with honor by Pope Hadrian IV.

When he came to the throne, Charlemagne was apparently a brawling, lecherous, and virtually illiterate chieftain. At first he continued the old Merovingian practice of moving about from one residence to another, as exigency or expediency might demand. So far as we know, his predecessors had built no palaces for themselves that would deserve the least consideration as works of architecture. After his second trip to Italy, however, Charles was moved to select for himself a capital city, in recognition of the fact that the governments of Rome and of Constantinople were unthinkable apart from an urban establishment.

He chose a place his father had liked, the town of Aachen (formerly a Roman spa called Aquisgranum) about forty miles from Cologne. There, in the 780s and '90s, he had built a stone palace, a school, and an ambitious royal chapel (consecrated by Pope Leo III in 805) which seems to have been inspired by San Vitale, of which it is a stocky and not-so-refined country cousin. Though largely encased within later Gothic additions, the greater part of the building still stands, serving as the core of the Cathedral of Aachen.

Recognizing the burden and stigma of his illiteracy, Charlemagne put himself under the tutelage of the clerics in his retinue and faced the task of learning Latin and even a little Greek. He encouraged the monastic scriptoria in his domain greatly to increase their production of manuscripts—an activity in which the Benedictines had been engaged since the founding of their order in the sixth century. A considerable number of Carolingian books have survived, and much scholarly effort has lately been devoted to determining the sources of their styles and to assigning them to one or another of the known scriptoria. Neither of those undertakings has met with much success, since the amount of evidential material that has come down to us, in comparison with what could have been known in the ninth century, is minutely small.

Charlemagne's scribes clearly had before them, as models of the illuminator's art, late Roman and early Byzantine books. Their manuscripts are often so handsome as to lead one to believe that a genuine renaissance was taking place in the art of painting. In fact, however, the figural illustrations in the typical Carolingian volume are limited to a few Evangelist portraits, in keeping with what had apparently been the common ancient practice of prefacing a text with a picture of its author. The Evangelists are often represented with remarkable vitality; yet one observes in many of these images (Fig. 24) a tendency (not unrelated to that of the Anglo-Celtic style) toward filling the framed field with busy detail and a gaudy array of colors, with the result that the image forms a rich two-dimensional fabric that works against the suggestion of a rounded figure within a spatial volume. The ineptitude with which the artist handles so simple a problem in perspective as that of rendering an open book resting on a lectern reveals to us, not that he was an ignorant or incompetent painter, but that he was indifferent toward the emotional concern or the philosophical presuppositions that underlay the kind of imagery he was turning to for a model—a concern for capturing an aspect of an observer's optical experience of the world and for setting a spatial stage for dramatic action. (Needless to say, there was no revival of the art of the drama in Charlemagne's day.) Sometimes the artist employs a

Figure 21. *Enthroned Christ.* From Gospels written by Godescalc for Charlemagne ca. 781. (Bib. nat., Paris: nouv. acq. lat. 1203). (Courtesy of Dr. Franz Stoedtner, Düsseldorf.)

F. 2

"landscape" setting, as in the Ebbo Gospels (Fig. 22); but though there are plants beside the Evangelist and trees and hills across the top of the page, there is no horizontal extension into depth, no ground plane, no spatial continuum. What few narrative images we find in Carolingian books cause us to suspect that they were copied from an earlier source by a scribe who was even less concerned with the old traditions of pictorial narration than was the artist whose work he was copying. They are highly reductive and tend toward a kind of symmetrical schematization that causes the over-all compositional diagram to take precedence over considerations of narrative sequence or of general intelligibility.

By far the most interesting and revealing illustrations that have survived from the Carolingian era are those of the Utrecht Psalter, a work that is thought to have been produced near Rheims around 825, that was taken to England, where it was admired and copied in the eleventh and twelfth centuries, and that eventually wound up in the library of the University of Utrecht in The Netherlands. The book is written in large, clear capitals, similar to those of the Vatican Virgil. Below each Psalm is an unframed horizontal "illustration" of its text, executed in brown ink and in an agitated and sketchy style like that of the Ebbo Gospels. Every picture is in the form of a panoramic landscape. One sees hills, trees, rivers, seas, cities inside their walls, palaces, churches, the Lord in the heavens, a profusion of angels, and hundreds of little figures of good men and bad, gesticulating frenetically as they give expression to the passionate urgency of the Psalmist's words. The visual scheme resembles that of the Odyssey Landscapes, a series of Roman wall paintings from the first century before Christ that show successive episodes from the Odyssey, acted out by vigorous little figures in the foreground and middle distance. Our Carolingian artist had probably seen a Roman book with similar illustrations; it is altogether possible that he had seen actual Roman frescoes, for at that time there were probably many ancient buildings, both in Rome and in Gaul, that had not yet fallen into ruins.

And yet how can one illustrate a book of poetic prayers? The Bible abounds in stories that can be visualized, even though the reader is never invited to do so by the language of the Hebrew text; but when David cries out, "The Lord is my light and my salvation; whom shall I fear?" one does not envision the Lord's providing David with light,

Figure 22. *St. Luke.* Gospel Book of Ebbo, Rheims, *ca.* 820. (Courtesy of Bibliothèque municipale, Epernay.)

F-3

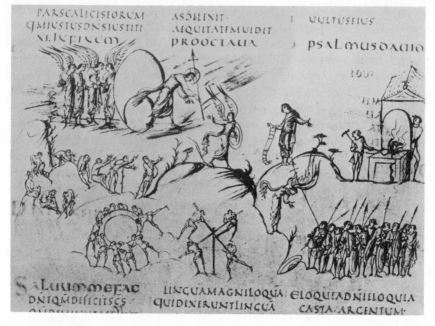

Figure 23. Psalm 12, Utrecht Psalter, Rheims (?), ca. 820 (Library, University of Utrecht, Script. Eccl. 484). (Courtesy of Dr. Franz Stoedtner, Düsseldorf.)

to say nothing of handing him a torch as he stands in front of a church-like building in a wide landscape. Yet this is precisely what we behold in the illustration to Psalm 27 in the Utrecht Psalter.

Since it is a short one, let us consider Psalm 12 (Fig. 23). In the upper portion of the image we see the Lord stepping out of his mandorla, suiting his action to the words, "Now will I arise, saith the Lord." Below him an angel extends a long spear in order to strike the mouth of a man: "The Lord shall cut off all flattering lips, and the tongue that speaketh proud things." In the upper right area we see a silversmith tending his furnace: "The words of the Lord are pure words: as silver tried in a furnace of earth, purified seven times." In the lower center section four men are walking about, pushing the arms of a turnstile: "The wicked walk on every side, when the vilest men are exalted." And so it goes. Every phrase that can suggest some kind of visual analogue is "illustrated" in some part of the panorama. The spatial sequence, however, does not—indeed, could not—correspond to the temporal sequence of the Psalmist's lines, in the way the Odyssey pictures follow the sequence of Homer's narrative.

Fascinating though they are, then, and brilliantly gifted though their artist was, the Psalter's illustrations betray a profound misunderstanding of the ancient landscape and narrative painting with which the Carolingian scribe was obviously familiar. Though he employed certain elements of ancient perspective, he did not share with the Roman artist a common attitude toward the experience of being either an observer or a performer: he had no awareness of his own location in space, wherefore his foreground figures are no larger than those on his "horizon"; he had no eye for the qualitative aspects of visual experience, such as the interplay of light and shadow; and although his figures are often wildly active, he shows no concern for that anatomical articulation of the human body by virtue of which the active figure is made to seem convincing and effective in both ancient and Renaissance art. A number of writers have spoken of the great emotional and even dramatic force of the illustrations; yet the fact of the matter is that while the Psalms vary widely in expressive mood (compare, for instance, the 22nd with the 23rd), the style and visual impact of the Carolingian images do not, but are as constant as the uncial script itself. One is reminded of Picasso's recent "variations" on compositions by Velasquez, Delacroix, and others: they, too, are far more agitated than are the paintings by the older artists, yet they are also far less expressive of human emotion—are as lacking as are the Utrecht Psalter sketches in that sense of a unified *occasion* that was so important both to Velasquez and to the Roman artist of the first century.

It is hard to know whether historical perspective helps or deceives us. We try to write with learned assurance about the art of the ninth century, yet we find it exceedingly difficult to fathom the implications of the painting that is being produced in our own day. It has been customary for forty years or more to praise Picasso, as the archetypal modern artist, for the warmly personal expressiveness of his paintings; but suddenly we discover that the outcome of the whole development he represents so well has been the production, by the "op," "primary structures," and "minimal" artists of the 1960s, of the most "objective" and inexpressive works that the world has known for centuries. Though the connections are more negative than positive—a matter of what is repudiated rather than of what is avowed—there is an odd link at this point with the art of the Utrecht Psalter; for it seems likely, at least, that its illustrations reflect an attitude of archaic literalness toward the meaning of the word. The artist tries to make the meaning of the Psalms "objectively" visible to the reader, without realizing that his visual inventions (the furnace, for instance, or the turnstile) destroy, by their very literalism, the rich metaphors in terms of which the Psalmist expresses himself. What is missing from his panoramic images is just that imaginative participation in the meaning of the text that we find in Roman illustration, or in the Biblical paintings of Rembrandt, but not in Carolingian art.

This literalistic or objectifying tendency finds expression in Carolingian architecture as well. Far more interesting than the Palace Chapel at Aachen was the Church of S. Riquier at Centula (near the modern French city of Abbeville). The building was destroyed long ago; what we know of its appearance comes to us by way of a seventeenth-century copy of an eleventh-century drawing. A monastery church, it was erected shortly before the year 800 by one of Charlemagne's most trusted advisers, the Abbot Angilbert.

S. Riquier is the first medieval church, so far as we know, in which exterior design takes precedence over interior design. The early basilicas and domical churches were like geodes: they were bare on the outside but richly adorned with shimmering materials on the inside, where the worshiper experienced astonishing effects of space and of light. There was preserved in such buildings that interior emphasis which had first been achieved by the Romans, in a development that was related to their taste for perspective vista in painting—and this, in turn, was

Figure 24. Restorational drawing (after Effmann) of Church of S. Riquier, Centula, ca. 798.   F- 5

bound up with their self-conscious awareness of the spatial context of a person's self-centered existence. Now the builders of S. Riquier imported fine materials from Italy in order to make their church a treasured and precious object; but it is reasonably clear that their principal concern was with its form, with its nature as a thing, rather than with experiences of vista (the decay of which concern is fully documented in works such as the Utrecht Psalter).

We have crossed the borderline at this point from a late-antique into an early-archaic mode of thinking. It is characteristic of virtually all the architecture of the archaic cultures of Egypt, Mesopotamia, and Greece that it stressed shapes rather than spaces, the thing itself rather than the experience of seeing and of moving about within the architectural object.

The meaning of S. Riquier, as it has been interpreted by Schapiro, is conveyed most obviously by its twin clusters of towers, which establish accents at the two ends of the building in an invention that is unprecedented, so far as we know. If we accept the proposition that architecture is an art of institutional symbolism, bearing ultimately upon the nature of the state, and if we inquire, then, as to the pertinency of S. Riquier's shape, we will inevitably be struck by the relation of its duality to a political development that came to fruition immediately after the building was dedicated—the coronation of Charlemagne by Pope Leo III, in old St. Peter's on Christmas Day in the year 800, as Emperor of the Holy Roman Empire. Though the circumstances that led up to this event are obscure, there is evidence to indicate that it had been in the making for many months prior to that fateful Christmas.

Charlemagne was then fifty-eight years old. By that time he had brought under his loose control almost all the lands over which the papacy had effective jurisdiction. Not only had he rescued Italy from Lombard domination, but he had brought thousands of Saxons into the church (by forced conversion and baptism!) in lands that had previously lain outside Christendom. Pope Leo's action amounted to an open recognition of what was already an accomplished fact: the existence of two coextensive monarchies in Europe, a secular one centered in Aachen and an ecclesiastical one centered in Rome, both of which claimed sovereignty over the entire population. Both owned land, levied taxes, enforced laws, issued edicts, built buildings. Needless to say, the possibilities of rivalry and conflict within this pattern of joint jurisdiction were unlimited, and they were fully realized in later generations, especially in the eleventh century; but what was achieved in Charlemagne's lifetime was a working partnership between two institutions

of the West (not Holy Roman Empire)

that were yet one, since they sustained one another and had the same members. This is the affirmation that is made in the shape of S. Riquier. As Pope Gelasius had expressed it in the 490s, "Two there are"—two authoritative institutions that had been given jurisdiction over different aspects of man's welfare in God's world. In radical contrast to Hagia Sophia, which culminates in a single central accent, the church at Centula is presided over by two great landmark forms, one at either end of the nave, or of the "ship," that contains the community of the faithful, lay and clerical alike. Its design is unified, but its unity is that of a harmonious and equable duality.

IV

Carolingian art continued to be produced throughout much of the ninth century, especially in the Western Kingdom. By the end of that century, however, Charlemagne's empire had disintegrated. There were two obvious reasons for its demise. In the first place, Frankish law required that all sons should inherit equal shares of their father's estate. When Charles died in 814, only one of his legitimate sons, Louis, was still alive; but Louis the Pious had three sons, and so the empire was divided into three parts, and as time went on it was subdivided still further. And, secondly, from the beginning of the ninth century onward, the empire was increasingly harried by ruthless new enemies: by the Northmen or Normans from Scandinavia, who attacked the western coasts and sent raiding parties deep into the kingdom, sacking cities and villages; by the Hungarians, who now appeared on the eastern frontiers; and by the Saracens from North Africa, who established strong bases on the Mediterranean coast of Europe, from which marauding bands penetrated even into the high Alps. Many cities that had endured since Roman times were now all but abandoned, their inhabitants driven to putting themselves under the protection of feudal lords, in whose rural strongholds there seemed to lie the only promise of security.

The years between 900 and 965 see perhaps the nadir of the economic and political breakdown that is referred to by the phrase "dark age"; it was the period of furthest removal from those aspects of civilized life we associate with *civitas*, or with the city, the period of greatest poverty, illiteracy, and isolation. Architecture came virtually to a standstill. And yet even such a time was capable of giving rise to a powerful art. The most telling inventions of the period are to be found in the *Beatus* manuscripts (copies of a popular commentary on the Apocalypse, written in the eighth century by the Spanish monk, Beatus of Liebana) which were produced in Mozarabic Spain. The greatest of these, the *Beatus of S. Sever*, is actually an eleventh-century copy of such a work, but it preserves intact the vivid and violent style of an earlier time.

It is significant, to begin with, that what captured the imagination in that dark time was the Apocalypse, with its ecstatic and unearthly imagery, its shattering evocation of visions of lightning and earthquake, of a raining of blood and fire, of the opening of the bottomless pit of hell and the emergence of the minions of Satan, of the universal destruction of the world by war and plague and famine and death. In some

F- 6

Figure 25. *Satan and his Locusts.* Beatus of S. Sever (B.N. lat. 8878), ca. 1050. (By permission of Bibliothèque nationale, Paris.)

ways the tendency of all West-European art from the fifth century onward had been world-negating rather than world-affirming. This tendency reaches its apogee in images such as that of *Satan and his Locusts* (Fig. 25) (cf. Rev. 9 : 1-11)—a brilliant pictorial invention in which the artist shows us, by means of a pattern of tumbling and dissonant irregularity against garish blocks of harshly complementary color (red against green, purple against yellow), the torments of the scorpion-stung sinners who "shall seek death and shall not find it; shall desire to die and death shall flee from them."

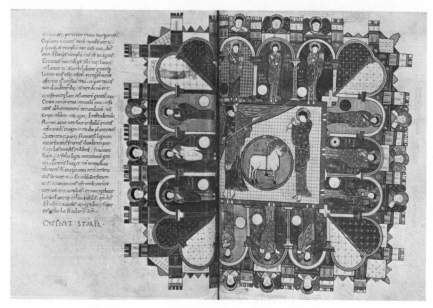

Figure 26. *Heavenly Jerusalem.* Beatus of S. Sever (B.N. lat. 8878), ca. 1050. (By permission of Bibliothèque nationale, Paris.)

P~7

At the opposite extreme is the regularity of the artist's image (Fig. 26) of the Heavenly Jerusalem (Rev. 21 : 10-23). The vision that came to John in the first century was characteristically Roman: he was carried up by an angel to the top of a high mountain, where he saw before him, laid out in all its vastness, a golden city that measured 12,000 furlongs, or about 1,500 miles, in perimeter. Its walls were made of precious stones, and each of its twelve gates was formed out of a single huge pearl. The vision is dominated throughout by the experiencing of light, luster, luminosity. A Van Eyck or an Altdorfer could scarcely have done justice to John's description; a Mozarabic scribe could not think in such terms at all. His city is laid out flat (like the pond in an Egyptian garden image); he gives us only a small, compact diagram—and, at that, not of a city but only of a four-walled, twelve-arched fortress which contains twelve men, fourteen angels, and the Lamb of God, rather than "the nations of them which are saved [who] shall walk in the light of it."

FOOTNOTES

page 39   [1]This mode of illustration is curiously similar to the one that has in recent years won universal acceptance among publishers of primary readers of the *Dick and Jane* variety. The new kind of unframed illustration is also associated with the elimination of dramatic narration in favor of something as blandly unpurposive as lacking in spiritual cogency as are the little domestic scenes in Figure 18. Broadly speaking, the problem of the *frame* is as perplexing for the modern artist as it was for the sixth-century illustrator.

Many years ago Meyer Schapiro observed the relationship between this art and certain kinds of modern painting which also derive from the artist's activity as such. The resemblance has only increased as we have gone from Pollock's webs to Jasper Johns' letters and numbers, and from those cryptic and indecipherable canvases to the "op art" patternings of Anuskiewicz and Vasarely, in a sequence of developments that have become steadily less expressive of dramatic feeling and more divorced from all experiences other than those of making and looking at paintings.

4

Romanesque Art

Here, as is often the case, the terminology of art history is itself a stumbling block. The word Romanesque looks as if it should mean "Roman-like"; but if it was ever intended to mean that, it was only in a derogatory sense, implying that the Romanesque is a degenerate and corrupted form of Roman art. A century and a half ago, when the word *Romanesque* was first employed, the art of classical antiquity may have seemed to provide men with a timeless standard of excellence by reference to which the merit of other styles could be judged; but we are no longer able to think in such terms today. Some scholars have equated the word *Romanesque* with *romance*, in the sense in which we speak of the *romance* languages; but if we were to use that term instead, as the French do, we would run into difficulties because of its kinship with *romantic* and even *romanticism*, terms which have little relevancy to Romanesque art. If there is any utility at all in our isolating and defining historical "periods" (and there may well be very little indeed!), then we should do better to call this one by a nonsense word— *Glig*, say—so as to avoid any suggestion of a one-word characterization.

Not only is it difficult to epitomize the sense of the art we call Romanesque; there is no firm consensus as to the chronological limits of the period. The word was once used to designate a span of some four or five hundred years, from the emergence of the Carolingian style until the flowering of the Gothic at the end of the twelfth century. With increasing art-historical specialization, it has come to be used now by many scholars to refer to a period of scarcely more than a single century—from about 1040 until about 1140. If the purpose of such restriction is to make the word applicable to a homogeneous body of material, the effort is in vain, for it is in the very nature of Romanesque art that it cannot be reduced to a formula or defined as a consistent "style"—unless, of course, one may choose to regard dissonant and disjunctive diversity as being of itself a unifying characteristic.

The era in question, which will here be defined as extending from about 960 until about 1160, sees a reversal of that disparagement of the world and of man's earthly existence that had become conventional after the fall of Rome. A depreciatory attitude toward the world had had a place in Christian thought from the beginning. Had not Jesus said, "Lay not up for yourselves treasures upon earth," and John, "Love not the world, neither the things that are in the world"? The stance became a cornerstone of the religious cosmology of the Dark Age and was duly institutionalized in monasticism—wherefore it was not to be set aside without a struggle. Romanesque art documents that struggle. It was conducted on many fronts and took many forms, but at every point it involved a reassessment of the Christian's relation to the world.

The struggle was not between the clergy and the laity, even though in some instances it may have taken that shape. Romanesque art is largely the product of the monastic church; and while it may at times address itself to the disaffected townsman, it reveals the presence within the monasteries themselves of attitudes that can best be described by the currently fashionable word *ambivalent.* Since monks were not the children of monks but had to be recruited from the adult laity, they inevitably brought with them into the cloister the ferment and restlessness that were abroad in the world in the eleventh and twelfth centuries. Moreover, to the extent that the monasteries were still important centers of learning, they were directly involved in that revitalization of intellectual life that was attended by the founding of universities, the appearance of the wandering scholars, the gaining of a new knowledge of ancient and Islamic thought, and the development of an attitude of skeptical inquiry.

They were involved with the world in other ways, as well. The earliest monasticism (from the Greek word *monos,* "alone") had been anchoritic: it had required of its adherents a withdrawal from society to the life of the lonely hermit. As the Roman state collapsed in the fifth and sixth centuries, anchoritism gave way to cenobitism: the model Christian was no longer the desert recluse but the perfect citizen-member of an ideal community, leading a totally disciplined life under vows of poverty, chastity, and obedience. By the year 1000, however, the monastic orders had come to possess great wealth, and because of their wealth they were frequently infected with laxity and corruption, with the characteristic sins of the "world." Having been given vast lands, together with the serfs who were bound to those lands, they were deeply immeshed in the economic and social structure of feudalized Europe.

But while the monasteries had their obvious reasons for wanting to maintain the *status quo*, they were also caught up in that new excitement about the world that found expression in pilgrimage, in crusading, in the opening of trade routes—in a general turning outward that had to contend with habits and traditions implanted during some four or five hundred years of turning inward, or away from the world.

And so the feelings of the monks (and of the laity, as well) were ambivalent, a mixture of affirmation and denial, of exuberance and repression, of expansiveness and constraint. A number of writers, such as Baltrusaitis and Focillon, have been struck with the importance of the *frame* as an aesthetic and organizing factor in Romanesque art. We could find no better point of departure for our consideration of the Romanesque than this, the frame; for no matter was of more compelling concern than that of limits, of containment, of context. Though nothing were more hazardous than to invent for ourselves an abstraction we

F - 8

Figure 27. *St. John.* Amiens Gospels (Municipal library, Amiens), *ca.* 1040. (Courtesy of Dr. Franz Stoedtner, Düsseldorf.)

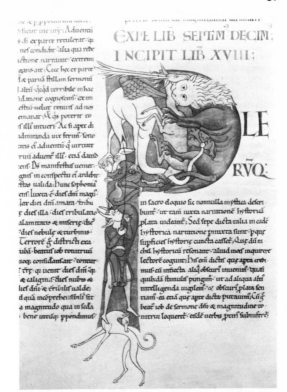

F-9

Figure 28. Initial letter, from Gregory's Commentary on Job (Bibliothèque de Dijon, Ms. 175). (Courtesy of Studio R. Remy, Dijon.)

could call "Romanesque man," we can easily imagine that many a work of Romanesque art was produced by a spiritual kinsman of the St. John we see in Figure 27. Legs crossed, arms crossed, wrapped in a knotty pattern of red, white, and black drapery lines, the saint sits, dour and self-entangled, within the too-narrow limits of an architectural frame, for all the world like some cloistered monk who had just been forbidden by his abbot to take up arms and march off to holy war in the Holy Land. It was such a monk, we fancy, who, as he returned dutifully to his task of making still another copy of Gregory's *Commentary on Job*, invented for the next capital letter he came to—it happened to be a *P*—the engagingly ferocious snarl of figures (lion, deer, dragon, devil, man, dog) reproduced in Figure 28. When he had finished it he felt better and cheerfully looked forward to the next initial, which would be even more hideously beautiful, he knew.

We observed in our last chapter that one of the symptomatic developments at the beginning of the Dark Age had been the abandonment of the Roman "window" frame in the making of illustrations, and that with the decline of the frame there went also a declining interest in narrative subject matter. Shortly before the end of the tenth century both frame and narration came back into vogue with astonishing vitality —witness the Easter morning scene (Fig. 29) from the Benedictional of St. Aethelwold, a manuscript that was produced at Winchester, in southern England, around 975.

St. Aethelwold was a Benedictine monk and an ardent reformer of monastic practice, which had become lax and ill-regulated in England because of the disruption of the country by the Danes. At the time

E- 1

Figure 29. *Maries at the Tomb.* Benedictional of St. Aethelwold, Winchester, ca. 975. (Brit. Mus. Add. Ms. 49598. By permission of the Trustees of the British Museum.)

the book was made, he was bishop of Winchester, which see he staffed with Benedictines who had been instructed by French monks in the proper performance of the liturgies of the church. This biographical detail is important, I believe, for there begins at this very time a development which quickly leads, by way of an embellishment and enrichment of the liturgy of which the "Winchester tropes" are one of the earliest examples, to the enactment of those "mysteries" in the church which mark the first step toward the revival of the drama in modern Europe. In fact, the oldest mystery play we know of is the *Quem*

quaeritis ("Whom seekest thou?"), an acting-out of the encounter between the angel and the holy women at the empty tomb on Easter
morning.

Scholars who like to look for the sources of manuscript imagery
have long ago observed a similarity between the Winchester style and
that of certain Carolingian works—in particular, the relation of the
agitated linearity of the figure drawing to that of the Utrecht Psalter,
and of the colorful acanthus border to such Rhenish works as the
Drogo Sacramentary. But though their observations are probably valid,
they contribute little to our understanding of Aethelwold's Benedictional. What matters here is not the source but the departure. Most obviously, the long drift away from narration has been decisively reversed.
The pivotal events in the life of Christ are here richly illustrated in an
original and forceful style.

Despite the destruction of monastic libraries by Danish invaders,
the Anglo-Celtic style of illumination must still have been familiar to
the British clergy, even as the late Roman style had been familiar to
the Anglo-Celtic scribes; but just as the latter had knowingly turned
away from Roman narrative painting, so now their own manner was
rejected in favor of one that has many links with Romano-Byzantine
tradition. One might argue, of course, that St. Aethelwold had simply
imported from the Continent a new set of "models" to replace those
the raiders had burned; but such an approach to the matter seems unduly
mechanical. While no one is quite sure what validity a cyclical theory
of history may possess, I think it worth keeping in mind that around
600 B.C., at the beginning of the archaic period in Greece, a lively art
of narrative painting superseded one of over-all patternization that had
combined conventionalized animal forms, both natural and fantastic, with
abstract geometrical shapes. So far as we know, there were no prototypes for this storytelling art, which E. H. Gombrich regards as the
crucial invention that determined the character of figural imagery in
the Graeco-Roman world for the following thousand years. It was the
painter of black-figure vases who first gave visual expression to the
Homeric idea that man is a performer of deeds within a temporal order
of things that has the coherency of a story or a play. As was observed
in Chapter 3, the setting-aside of this idea marks the beginning of the
Dark Age. In the Romanesque period it reemerges, albeit gradually
and in the face of resistance.

Carolingian that he was, the painter of the Drogo Sacramentary
had been content to insert minutely small narrative scenes within the
outlines of his acanthus-leaved capital letters. He had lost all sense of
the dependency of pictorial narration on *context*. In Roman painting,

as in that of the Renaissance, the setting that supported narrative was replete with architecture, furnishings, garden and landscape elements, light and shadow, and subtly modulated color harmonies—a repertory of which we find only the rudimentary beginnings in archaic black-figure painting. Now the Romanesque is also an archaic art, with formal mannerisms in the rendering of drapery and the figure that are often surprisingly similar to those we encounter in the painting and sculpture of sixth-century Greece. However, because some knowledge of Roman illustration had survived throughout the Dark Age, the Romanesque artist could incorporate into his archaic style a half-understood vocabulary of complex figure poses, richly articulated drapery patterns, intricate figure groupings, and architectural props, all of which we see in Figure 29.

And yet the essential factor of Roman illustration, the spatial continuum, is missing. Everything still lies on the page and in front of the page, even as had been the case in the Book of Kells. But the artist did perceive the necessity of there being a context, the vigorous "reality" of which would sustain what he evidently felt to be the emotional significance of the scene. He could not convey that significance by genuinely dramatic means; in fact, such expression was not to be fully achieved in European painting until Leonardo had completed his *Last Supper* some five hundred years later—which painting is as far removed from the Benedictional of St. Aethelwold as is *Hamlet* from *Quem quaeritis*. But in this new and dynamic relationship between text and illustration, between image and frame, between action and context, we see the dawning of a new era in western art. For this was no "palace renaissance," soon to be snuffed out for want of a real basis in the economic, political, and religious life of its day. What took root in the Romanesque period was destined to grow and to flourish for some nine hundred years.

The Benedictional is an early Romanesque (some would say proto-Romanesque) manuscript. So as to make clear the direction of stylistic development in the period, let us compare it with a late example (one that could be called proto-Gothic)—namely, the Morgan Leaf (Fig. 30), which was also made in Winchester, about two hundred years after St. Aethelwold's time. On this single page from a lost Bible there are six scenes that take us from the early youth to the old age of King David, or from the slaying of Goliath to the death of Absalom. We see at a glance that the artist now has at his command a far greater repertory of pictorial devices: he employs varied poses in order to express steadfastness, aggressiveness, dismay, anger, alarm, and grief; and though he has no comparable vocabulary of facial expressions, he dif-

E-2

Figure 30. *Story of David.*
The Morgan Leaf, Winches-
ter, ca. 1180. (By permission of the Pierpont Morgan
Library, New York.)

ferentiates the members of his "cast" by making some men clean-shaven,
some short-bearded, some long-bearded, some red-headed, some bru-
nette, some gray-haired, some with hats, some hatless. He must have
spent many hours in executing the frame around the image: it is bound-
ed by thin strips of gold leaf and contains twenty-eight colorful semi-
circles, each of which is composed of a single strap that has been folded
fifty times to form an elaborate three-dimensional fret pattern. Yet the
painted frame is much less important than it was in the Benedictional,
for the context with which the artist is seriously concerned lies within
the scenes rather than around them. He uses several devices for putting
a ground line under his figures (something that is quite lacking in
Fig. 29); he places the two central scenes within, rather than in front
of, an architectural setting; and he puts square panels of a contrasting
color behind the other four scenes in order to make it plain that the
figures do not simply lie on the flat page but are in front of something
that lies behind the plane of the picture itself—a very small step toward
a landscape background, as Schapiro has pointed out, but a step, none-

theless. The panels have a temporal function, also, in that they help to isolate successive scenes which are not otherwise separated from one another. A few elements still project in front of the picture frame, others disappear behind it. The colors are strong and bright (yellow, blue, red, gold, and white predominate), so that one still sees the page first and foremost as a rich and agitated picture-surface. The effect is one of shallow relief rather than of vista, in which respect the work is still akin to the Benedictional of St. Aethelwold.

II

This brings us to another of the primary innovations of Romanesque art: the resurgence of the art of sculpture, which had been moribund during the Dark Age. Toward the end of the eleventh cen-

Figure 31. *Isaiah*. Church of St. Mary, Souillac, *ca.* 1120 (Courtesy of Archives photographiques, Paris.)

tury there began a period of about two hundred years during which (as had been the case in the sixth and fifth centuries B.C. in Greece) stone sculpture was used profusely for the adornment of stone buildings. There could be no more obvious manifestation of the "turning outward" that distinguishes Romanesque from earlier art. The flattened, weightless, static figures of the Byzantine mosaicist had typically been placed in the dimly lit hollows of the domes and half-domes of the central church, where their effect was to minimize the significance of the physical reality of the human body, with its power to act forcefully in a world of substantial objects. By carving the figure in stone, and on the outside of the church where it faced the busy town, the Romanesque sculptor reasserted that significance—though ambivalently, as we should have expected.

B-10

Consider, for instance, the image of Isaiah (Fig. 31) from the now-dismembered portal of the Benedictine Church of St. Mary at Souillac, in southwestern France. The figure is carved in high relief, yet it seems curiously emaciated, its rotundity overwhelmed by the excited linear pattern that plays over and around the form. The prophet holds out a scroll on which, in all probability, there was once painted a text; indeed, the whole figure may have been brightly painted in the twelfth century. It seems to move invitingly toward the entrance, but at the same time its head is thrown back in the opposite direction so that it appears to advance and to retreat simultaneously. Standing in that portal, the medieval villager may have had similar feelings; for at its center, separating the two doors into the church, there once stood the celebrated Souillac pillar (Fig. 32) —a 10-foot trumeau that is carved into as strange and grotesque a form as is to be found in the whole corpus of Romanesque art. It is composed of interlocking lions and griffons, between whose crossed bodies there tumble the forms of animals and of men, both savagely bitten by the monsters. The pillar had no more Christian signifi-cance, to the best of our knowledge, than had the grotesque initial P of Figure 28. It affirmed something about the darkness and turmoil of man's existence, but it did so with exuberant inventiveness and force: it is extraordinarily positive in its negativity.

The sculpture that adorns the Roman-esque church is usually concentrated with-in and around the entrance to the building, where it commonly makes the doorway both fascinatingly attractive and awesome-ly disturbing. This is the point at which one steps within the frame of the building itself, passing from the infinite diversity and precariousness of the temporal world into the precincts of an institution that claimed to transcend that world and to make available to man an eternal serenity —or, to those who would not accept its terms, eternal torment. It would appear

Figure 32. Pillar, Church of St. Mary, Souillac, ca. 1120. (Courtesy of Archives photo-graphiques, Paris.)

F - 11

from the sculptural evidence that that choice between terrestrial tur-
bulence and paradisiacal repose was not an easy one for the twelfth-
century Christian to make; for the doorway is interpreted more often
as a point of crisis than of juncture, of separation than of union.

Apocalyptic themes are frequently depicted in the sculptured tympana of Romanesque doorways. The most telling of these subjects was
the Last Judgment, in which the separation of the damned from the
elect could be rendered with excruciating delight. By far the most
powerful representation of the subject is to be found at the entrance
to the church of S. Lazare at Autun, in Burgundy. The tympanum
(Fig. 33) was carved in the 1120s by a sculptor who gave evidence of
a new kind of self-awareness among artists by signing his work—*Gislebertus hoc fecit*. The image is dominated by a frontal and implacable
figure of Christ, who offers us a choice between heaven on his right
and hell on his left. It would have been logical and conventional for
the sculptor to have shown the weighing of the souls in the center of
the image, as in the tympanum at Conques; but that would have neces-
sitated its being placed in the narrow space beneath Christ's feet, wherefore the participants in the weighing would have been very small, as

Figure 33. *Last Judgment* tympanum. Church of S. Lazare, Autun,
ca. 1125. (Courtesy of Archives photographiques, Paris.)

F-12

Figure 34. Pentecost. Church of the Madeleine, Vézélay, ca. 1125.
(Courtesy of Archives photographiques, Paris.)

F-13

they are at Conques. For Gislebertus, however, the struggle between
angels and devils for possession of the essentially Jeckyll-and-Hyde-ish
souls of men was too important an aspect of the theme to be consigned
to the fringes of his image; and so he puts the scales on Christ's left,
where the weighing occupies more than half of the area that would
otherwise have been given over to the torments of the wicked. The
composition is thereby given a secondary axis which competes with
that of the symmetrical Christ figure, making for a kind of dissonance
that was meat and drink to the Romanesque artist. The tympanum
abounds in thrusting, jutting, angular, unstable forms; it possesses nothing whatever of the legalistic decorum that would become characteristic
of Gothic images of the same subject less than a century later. Not the
hell scene only but the entire relief seems to flicker in seething torment
before our eyes.

At about the same time, in the nearby town of Vézélay, another
Burgundian sculptor was chiseling out an equally renowned tympanum
(Fig. 34), in which the juncture between the church and the world was
treated, in a different way. His subject was the Pentecost—that is, the
descent of the Holy Spirit, coming with "a sound from heaven as of

a rushing mighty wind," to touch Christ's disciples with "tongues like as of fire" and to inspire them to go forth to preach the Gospel to the world. In the center of the tympanum hovers the flattened, apparitional figure of Christ, agitated as by a rushing wind, from whose extended hands pass rays of light that touch the heads of the apostles, causing them to be seized with an ecstatic frenzy and to "speak with other tongues, as the Spirit gave them utterance."

All around this scene are groups of little figures representing the men "of every nation under heaven" to whom the church had to extend its mission. Here the artist beguiles us with the marvels which, according to the legendary geography of the Middle Ages, lay in store for the traveler (merchant, missionary, or crusader) as he ventured into the remotest corners of the earth; for there he would meet dog-headed people, pig-snouted people, big-eared people—would see wonders about which he could tell his children and his grandchildren as long as he lived. And yet the little scenes of adventurous encounter do themselves form a heavy frame around the Pentecostal vision, and the whole image is set deep inside the architectural framework of the church building, above a doorway that leads not out into the world but into the abbey church of a Benedictine monastery. Moreover, the relation of that monastery to the world around it was not marked by Christian piety and charity: time and again throughout the twelfth century the citizens of Vézélay rose up in armed revolt against the rule of their monastic overlords, and each time the revolt was brutally crushed by the abbot and his feudal supporters. The message of the tympanum was ambivalent, to say the least.

The doorway is not the only point of tension in the Romanesque church. Inside the building the various joints and connections in the fabric of the architectural structure are commonly accented, as Schapiro has observed, with bits of entangled ornamentation or with clutches of figures that may illustrate a Biblical story or that may simply be, like the Souillac pillar, an outcropping of violence or of fantasy for its own sake. Hundreds of figurated Romanesque capitals have been preserved, no two of which are alike—though in a great many of them there are preserved the basic elements of the Roman Corinthian capital (Fig. 35). In antiquity the chief purpose of the classical orders, it would seem, had been to declare the equality of the functioning members of a building, to affirm the reign of law and of reason, of decorous normality, in whatever pertained to the state. That has generally been the purport of orderly columniation ever since. Only in the Romanesque period is that traditional meaning typically rejected; only then does one find long colonnades in which all the capitals are different, each having its own

Figure 35. *Monsters.* Capitals from Church of S. Pierre, Aulnay, France, ca. 1150. (Courtesy of Archives photographies, Paris.) F-14

shape and content. An "inflammation of the joints" accompanies a pro-liferation of the number of members, and of junctures between and among members, in the framework of the Romanesque building. The sculptor heightens our awareness of the architect's obsession with the problem of binding many separable and disparate members into a whole.

III

In the same years that saw a renewal of artistic activity in Win-chester—that is, in the 960s and '70s—there was taking place in Germany a far more ambitious revival of the arts and of architecture under a new dynasty of Saxon kings, the second of whom, Otto I, was crowned Emperor of the Holy Roman Empire in 962. But though Otto was nominally Charlemagne's successor, his kingdom was smaller than, and different from, that of the great Frank. Between the fall of the Caro-lingians and the rise of the Ottonians Europe had been feudalized. Charlemagne and his successors had often rewarded their faithful re-tainers by putting them in charge of extensive lands whose revenues they could enjoy for life. Contrary to the emperor's intention, however, such benefices commonly became feudal estates that were handed down to the heirs of the original recipients. By the middle of the tenth century those heirs had come to regard themselves as independent princes, and they resisted the demands of the Saxon upstarts who claimed to have authority over them; wherefore the emperors, finding themselves often at odds with the feudal lords, turned for support, instead, to their ec- clesiastical lords—to the bishops who governed many of the important cities of the empire and to the abbots who controlled large estates. Since churchmen had no heirs, there was no danger of their coming to regard their offices or titles as hereditary possessions. Seeing that it was only by filling these positions with his own men that he could maintain control over his factious kingdom, Otto the Great had aligned the church with his Saxon monarchy long before he was anointed Em- peror. In keeping with that policy, he appointed his brother Bruno to be Duke of Lotharingia and Archbishop of Cologne and his bastard son Wilhelm to be Archbishop of Mainz, while other descendants later became bishops, abbots, and abbesses.

Two aspects of the situation, it would seem, encouraged the Otto- nian emperors to look to "caesaropapist" Constantinople for their image of the state and for models in matters of art. In the first place, if the emperor's power was to be derived from and exercised through the church, it was necessary that his own office be endowed with sacred significance of the highest order. By the year 1000 it was possible for Otto III (whose mother, Theophano, was a Byzantine princess, daugh- ter of the emperor Romanus II) to have himself represented (Fig. 36) as the earthly counterpart of Christ himself: he is shown to be lifted up in a mandorla, flanked by the symbols of the Evangelists, crowned by the hand of God himself, and paid homage to by both secular and ecclesiastical princes. As John Beckwith observes, no Byzantine emperor would have gone so far, even though *christomimesis* was wholly a By- zantine idea.

Secondly, the emperors' reliance upon their bishops, whose power and position had since Roman times been identified with a city, gave added prestige to cities and all that pertained to urban life, in opposi- tion to that ruralization of political power that had proceeded apace from the mid ninth century onward. Charlemagne had recognized the importance of having a capital city; but Aachen was scarcely more than a palace city, just as the emperor's revival of the arts constituted only a palace renaissance. The strengthening of the cities that took place in Ottonian times had deeper roots and grew out of a more com- pelling need. Otto III built for himself a palace on the Aventine Hill,

Figure 36. *Glorification of Otto III.* Gospels of Otto III, *ca.* 1000. (Courtesy of Cathedral Treasury, Aachen.)

F-15

where he dreamed of restoring Rome to its ancient magnificence—of making it a worthy rival of The City, of whose splendor he must have been told by his mother, who had grown up in the Sacred Palace itself.

But there were troubles ahead. The Roman nobility, who had come to regard the election of popes as their own prerogative, resented the Saxon presence in their midst, and they were joined by churchmen in other lands (especially the abbots of Cluny) in protesting against Germanic control of the papacy. That control broke down in the 1040s, whereafter the popes sought to deny the emperors the right to appoint bishops and to invest them with ecclesiastical authority. The bitter struggle over the right of investiture—without which the emperors could not have held the empire together—reached its height during the papacy of Gregory VII, who excommunicated Henry IV because of his refusal to yield and compelled the emperor to humble himself before papal authority at Canossa in the winter of 1077.

It was in the midst of this contentious ferment, then, that there developed the vigorous Ottonian style of manuscript painting and the powerful Romanesque architecture of the Rhineland. The manuscript

style was developed in a small number of monastic scriptoria, of which
the most important were those at Reichenau, Trier, and Cologne. While
it is based chiefly on Carolingian prototypes, it contains elements that
could have been drawn only from Early Christian and from contemporaneous Byzantine art. We can easily see, for instance, that the
painter of the *Codex Egberti* (Fig. 37) had been looking at images
such as are to be found in the *Vatican Virgil* and in the mosaics of
Sta. Maria Maggiore. No less than the maker of the Benedictional of
St. Aethelwold, he was strongly attracted to narrative themes and came
surprisingly close, at times, to recapturing the illustrational usages of
late Roman painting. But though narrative images abound in Ottonian
art, this master's work was exceptional; most of his contemporaries and
successors preferred a background of pure gold, in the Byzantine manner, and were often at their best in dealing with ideational rather than
storytelling themes. Among the best examples of this type are the Evangelist portraits from the Gospels of Otto III. In Figure 38 we see a
fanatical Matthew, seated on a celestial arc within a circular mandorla
of light. Above and below him appear a number of fiery discs, reminiscent of Ezekiel's wheels, which contain bust-length images of six

Figure 37. *Nativity and Annunciation to Shepherds.* Codex Egberti, Trier or Reichenau, ca. 985. (Courtesy of
Trier Municipal Library.)

Figure 38. *St. Matthew.*
Gospels of Otto III (Baye-
rische Staatsbibliothek, Mu-
nich, Cod. lat. 4453), ca.
990. (By permission of Baye-
rische Staatsbibliothek.)

angels and of five Old Testament figures from whom Matthew drew
inspiration—Isaiah, Hosea, Joel, Amos, and Abraham, all of whom wear
jeweled crowns and, like Matthew, a garment of royal purple. Since
the background outside the arch is also purple and inside the arch, of
gold, the effect of the whole is as unmistakably regal as that of the
mosaic in the apsidal dome of San Vitale. Yet it is distinctly Romanesque; for unlike that early Byzantine work it contains a series of frames
within frames and is at the same time charged with an apocalyptic
energy and excitement that seem to burst the limits of those frames.

In this respect the portrait of Matthew rather resembles the Rhenish church architecture of the eleventh and twelfth centuries, which
is heavy-walled and fortress-like, on the one hand, and outward-thrust-
ing, aggressively salient, on the other. Like the figure of Matthew, the
façade of the Abbey Church of Maria Laach (Fig. 39) stares at us,
arms upraised, full of repressed excitement—a church that was begun
immediately before the launching of the First Crusade and that seems
permeated with the fanatical militancy that inspired that enterprise in
the 1090s.[1] The architect, like the painter, was fascinated with frame-
making: notice how he has multiplied the number of shafts and mold-

g- $4

Figure 39. Façade, Abbey Church of Maria Laach, 1093-1156. (Courtesy of Ars Liturgica, Maria Laach.)

ings so as to divide the walls of the church into many closed panels, and how he has then created dissonant effects by placing certain wall openings in off-center positions within those panels. A similar effect results from his putting an eight-sided pyramidal roof over each of his six-paneled stair towers, so that the rhythmic accents of the one do not coincide with those of the other. A more strident cacophony is produced by the opposition between the large rectangular and small cylindrical towers at one end of the building and the large octagonal and small square towers at the other end.

Here, as elsewhere in the Rhineland, the architect has plainly derived his basic form from that most important of all Carolingian inventions in architecture, the six-towered church of S. Riquier at Centula (Fig. 24). In Angilbert's church, however, the eastern and western sets of towers were alike, while in the Rhenish churches— Maria Laach, Speyer, Worms, Mainz, Trier, and others—the two clusters of towers are never alike. It is hard to say why this is the case. One is tempted, of course, to argue that it reflects the fact that church and state, pope and emperor, were no longer in harmonious agreement as they had been in the year 800; but that is too easy, for no architect would have associated one set of towers with the state and the other with the church, nor would he have thought it his function in life to "express" an inimical relationship between the institutions that jointly sponsored the erection of such buildings. It is too easy, also, to fall back upon ideas of *Zeitgeist* or of *Kunstwollen,* as if the artist did not have to think about such matters at all but automatically produced dissonant works in a dissonant age. Rather than to rely on such lame devices, we should do better to say that we do not know.

And yet, when we contemplate Gruber's restoration of the cathedral precinct of Worms to its twelfth century dimensions (Fig. 40), we can perhaps sense what it was the architect was after. Worms had been the site of a Roman fort on the Rhine, was later a barbarian capital and an important Merovingian town. Charlemagne had a palace there,

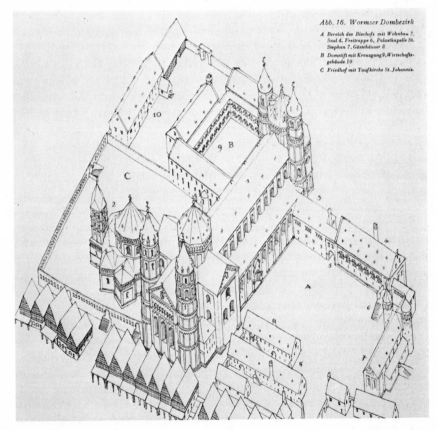

Figure 40. Cathedral Precinct of Worms, restored to twelfth-century condition. (From: Gruber, K., *Die Gestalt der Deutschen Stadt.* By permission of Georg D. W. Callwey Verlag, München.)

and from that time onward the bishops of Worms became increasingly powerful officials. They supported the early Ottonian emperors, who had increased the wealth of the diocese. During the investiture controversy of the eleventh century, however, the bishops demolished the palace in Worms and allied themselves with the papacy; but the townsmen sided with the emperor, who granted them commercial privileges in return for their support.

A new factor now enters the picture: the growing strength of the bourgeoisie. It would sometimes happen during the Dark Age that a few merchants would settle, for security's sake, at the gates of a bishop's stronghold, would pay him taxes for the right to do business, and would submit to episcopal regulation. By the beginning of the twelfth century, however, the burghers had become so numerous and so prosperous as to feel that they could dispense with the bishop's protection, and they began to resist his exactions. Between the 1060s and the 1140s, town after town, especially in France, rebelled against feudal domination and in many cases won charters of independence from their overlords.

It was in the midst of this three-sided conflict, then, involving emperor, bishop, and businessman, that the Cathedral of Worms was rebuilt in its present shape. The establishment resembles a self-sufficient monastery or feudal palace, its various functions gathered around walled courtyards. The bishop, who owned lands around the city and was himself a feudal lord of considerable power, had to make that power evident, both to the burghers and to the now-weakened emperors. One must bear it in mind, too, that the bishop controlled the administration of the sacraments of the church, which were conceived in the Middle Ages to possess an efficacy so objective, so external in nature, as to border virtually on the theurgic. The great, somber, militant church building, which towered over the city of Worms and had to be entered by passing through the courtyard of the bishop's palace, was deliberately designed, it would seem, to make the townsman mindful of the bishop's ultimate strength, which resided in his power to *shut out*—the power of interdict and of excommunication.

The lines were drawn differently in different places. In France the early Capetian kings were weaker than the Ottonian emperors, and the struggle over investiture was less rancorous; yet many a French Romanesque church has strongly contrasted eastern and western towers and a harsh, angular profile. What such shapes may have meant to churchmen we can only surmise from such bits of evidence as, say, the interpretation of the story of the Tower of Babel that we find on the frescoed ceiling of the church of S. Savin-sur-Gartempe (Fig. 41). In later versions, such as Peter Bruegel's, the image is dominated by the preposterous tower; but at S. Savin the artist stresses the opposition between the large figure of God on the left and that of King Nimrod on the right, the latter promoting, the former opposing the construction of a city, in dissonant terminal accents like those of the Cathedral of Worms.

In Norman England, on the other hand, church and crown were allied for many years after the Conquest in an efficiently centralized administration which worked to suppress the power of the feudal barons (who, in a reactionary move, regained certain of their old rights by

Figure 41. *Tower of Babel. S. Savin-sur-Gartempe, ca.* 1110. (Courtesy of Archives photographiques, Paris.) F - 16

forcing King John to sign the Magna Carta of 1215). King William and his heirs planted great churches at key points in their kingdom in order to make it plain, it would appear, that the Norman power had come to stay. Those buildings (Durham, Ely, Peterborough, Romsey, Gloucester, Tewkesbury, St. Albans, Norwich, and others) are in some respects more like the Gothic cathedrals of the thirteenth century than like the Romanesque churches of either France or Germany: they are imperial halls, enormously heavy still, but clearly articulated and free, for the most part, of the curious ambivalencies that are characteristic of so much Romanesque art.

In the Cathedral of Durham (Fig. 42) we see fully achieved something toward which Romanesque architects had been working, by way of a series of inventions we cannot enumerate here, for more than a century: the fully vaulted, materially homogeneous church interior. Carolingian and early Ottonian churches had had wooden ceilings (grievously subject to destruction by fire) that were carried on comparatively flat and simply perforated stone walls. Gradually the wall structure was transformed into a richly sculptured fabric of arches, pillars, piers, columns, colonnettes, and moldings, and the two walls of the nave were more and more closely linked, first by diaphragm arches and then by increasingly complex patterns of vaulting. In order to understand this development we should keep it in mind that, as has already been sug-

Figure 42. Nave interior, Cathedral of Durham, 1093-1133. (Courtesy of Dr. Franz Stoedtner, Düsseldorf.)

E-3

gested, the church building is itself a frame—one whose membering and whose system of connections have a direct bearing, we may reasonably suppose, upon the problem to which the church had more and more to address itself, that of maintaining certain conceptions of orderly subordination and containment in the face of growing restlessness and disaffection.

While William was superintending the development of his "Roman aqueduct" style of construction (as in the Abbaye aux Hommes in Caen, 1064), quite another atypical and in some ways proto-Gothic kind of Romanesque was taking shape in Italy—to be specific, in certain of the commercial cities that had already by the middle of the eleventh century achieved that proudly independent status we ordinarily associate with the Gothic cathedral towns and with the city-states of the Renaissance. The most celebrated examples of what I have in mind are to be found in two churches that were begun in the same year, 1063: the Cathedral of Pisa and the Church of San Marco in Venice. Though they are totally unlike in form, the one a basilican hall and the other a five-domed church in the Byzantine manner, they are similar in meaning: both buildings were erected as symbols of the defiant pride and ambitious self-confidence of a city.

Pisa had been an important naval base in Roman times. Hadrian had built a palace there in the second century. That Roman heritage was never forgotten in Pisa, any more than it was in Rome or Florence or Milan. When, therefore, in 1061 the Pisans seized a rich haul of booty from the Saracens in Palermo, they chose to use their treasure to restore to the city something of its ancient dignity. And so they salvaged many large columns from among the Roman ruins north of the city and built for themselves a 330-foot, five-aisled basilica (Fig. 43) that was worthy of being compared with the great fourth-century churches of Rome. Like them, it is composed, inside and out, of a large number of small parts that follow one another in quick succession and are nowhere forced into hierarchical groupings or closely knit patterns of subordination of the kind we see in Norman England. Close to the cathedral stand three other buildings: a circular baptistry (1153), in which children were initiated into the community; the leaning campanile (1174), which, rising to a height of 179 feet, dominated the skyline of the city; and the Campo Santo (1278), a cloistered burying ground where the dead could be laid to rest in earth that had been brought by ship from the Holy Land. The role of the church in ordering the life of the city and of the citizen was never more lucidly proclaimed than it is in these handsome marble buildings, so classical in appearance that one could

Figure 43. Cathedral of Pisa, with Baptistry and Campanile, 1063 *et ff.* (Courtesy of Dr. Franz Stoedtner, Düsseldorf.)

Pisa !

almost imagine them to have been designed by a Brunelleschi or an Alberti.

San Marco (Fig. 44) is conventionally dealt with, in books of this sort, under the general heading of Byzantine art—and logically enough, since the building is based directly upon one of Justinian's churches (now destroyed) in Constantinople and is more profusely decorated with mosaics than any Eastern church we know of. The significant question, however, pertains not to form but to meaning. The Venetians of 1063 were not members of the Greek Orthodox church and were not especially interested, so far as we know, in either the theological or the political principles which Justinian's domical architecture was designed to body forth. But they did envy Constantinople—so much so that they conspired in 1204 to divert the Fourth Crusade to the unsavory business of sacking and plundering that noble Christian city. Byzantium was known the world over for her church architecture; nothing proclaimed her greatness more cogently. How could Venice consider herself a rival of The City if she had no comparable buildings? Plainly she could not—wherefore San Marco.

While the church is Byzantine in style, then, it is Romanesque in date and in motivation. One has only to look at its mosaic decorations (especially those of the narthex) to see that the Venetians were as much preoccupied with the representation of lively events as were the painters of Winchester and of Reichenau; their taste did not much incline toward the stately, hierarchical themes of Ravenna and of Constantinople. Unlike the Byzantine churches of the East, moreover, San Marco is lavishly embellished on the exterior—and this, again, is typically a Romanesque manifestation. Yet it goes beyond that style period: in the lavishness and elegance of its decorations and above all in the

Figure 44. Façade, Church of San Marco, Venice, 1063 *et ff.* (From: Ongania, F., *Calli e Canali in Venezia*, Venice, 1890.)

importance that is accorded its great portals, which open onto the Piazza and welcome into the church the city's populace, it closely approaches, in purpose and meaning, the Gothic cathedrals of the following century.

FOOTNOTES

[1]To some readers it may seem farfetched to compare the façade of a large church with a book illustration only 13 inches high. Yet it must be kept in mind that even though we know nothing about the design procedures of the Romanesque

architect, every building first took shape, as is still the case, in a drawing of some kind. All such drawings in the eleventh century would certainly have been elevational, as is the image of Matthew. In the beginning, the façade of Maria Laach existed only as a small diagram. Our knowledge of the work of later architects makes it clear that the style of a builder's drawings cannot be divorced from the general state of image-making in his day. We may take it for granted, then, that the Benedictine architect of the abbey church was conversant with eleventh-century Rhenish manuscript painting, and that his basic ideas about the expressiveness of shapes and about compositional diagramming would have been similar to the painter's.

5

Again, a troublesome term. Part of the difficulty lies in the word itself. Needless to say, the style that superseded the Romanesque owed nothing at all to the Goths, who had disappeared from the European scene during the Dark Age. The word was applied to the style by Renaissance Italians who thought it barbaric and uncultivated, the invention of ignorant men beyond the Alps. Later the word lost its abusive meaning and came to be accepted as a neutral name for a period in the history of architecture that reached its highest development in the thirteenth century and was itself superseded by Renaissance classicism at different times in different countries.

All this need cause us little difficulty. Harder to deal with are the interpretative ideas that have come to be associated with the style during the past two hundred years—ideas that underlay the Gothic Revival of the nineteenth century, because of which movement one sees Gothic churches in hundreds of American cities today. The revival was compounded, it would seem, of two quite different attitudes toward medieval architecture. In the mid eighteenth century, when the Gothic novel was in vogue, Gothic buildings (especially if they happened to be in ruins) were thought to embody a romantic mysteriousness and organic vitality that were the antithesis of, and served as an antidote to, the mechanistic rationalism of the Enlightenment and later of industrialism. Something of this view persisted well into the twentieth century: it was the romantic interpretation of the Gothic that appealed to the German Expressionists and to critics such as Wilhelm Worringer.

In the last years of the eighteenth century the style came to be viewed in altogether another way. After the revolutions of the 1780s it served, especially in England, as a primary symbol of an historical tradition of which all the people of the nation were heirs and in which they all participated—a heritage so unifying as to render meaningless such revolutionary and divisive notions as that of the class struggle. Beginning with Wyatt's restoration of the Cathedral of Salisbury in the years between the American and French revolutions, scores of medieval churches were refurbished, in a wave of activity that reached its height during the 1840s (which saw the high-water point of revolutionary ferment, also) with the completion of the half-built Cathedral of Cologne, the virtual rebuilding of the Cathedral of Paris by Viollet-le-duc, and the erection of many stately Gothic buildings, such as the Houses of Parliament, all in defense of the idea of the historical continuity of the state. Architects and historians of this persuasion were inclined to stress, not the emotionality of the Gothic but the lucid rationality of its structural system, which was conceived to depend upon a perfectly harmonious equilibrium between the "thrusts" and "counterthrusts" of its various arcuated components.

The cathedral was pictured, moreover, as having been created by a host of anonymous artisans—masons, carpenters, sculptors, tapestry weavers, workers in stained glass—who collaborated in spontaneous and unstudied unanimity, with the result that the building became the very embodiment of the Christian spirit of its age. The superior virtue of anonymous craftsmanship, as compared with the "fine" art of the celebrated geniuses of Renaissance and later times, was affirmed by the leaders of the Arts and Crafts Movement in England, whence the doctrine spread to the Continent in the early 1900s. It has had its greatest impact on the modern world by way of the Bauhaus, where, in the wake of the disaster of World War I, it was hoped that the unaffected and anonymous craftsman-architect could learn to design buildings and other artifacts so appropriate to our own age that they would both express and engender a new *Zeitgeist,* thereby bringing together into harmonious unity, as the cathedral was believed to have done in the Middle Ages, the ill-assorted strands of contemporary life.

Yet we should be badly mistaken if we were to suppose that there existed a direct correspondence between the architecture and the "life" of the Gothic era, for it was anything but a time of social concord. As one historian puts it, speaking of the period from the middle of the twelfth to the middle of the thirteenth century:

Anarchy and violence had so deeply saturated the life of society that the success of monarchical authority was difficult and, in part at least, ephemeral. The Middle Ages had been an era of brutality. The nobility considered war as a normal condition of existence for a man of noble birth. . . . At the beginning of the thirteenth century, this anarchy seemed irremediable, for the French baron was master in his own house . . . [and] didn't allow the royal officers to enter his dominions. . . .

The lower clergy were much too coarse to be able to influence men to respect one another. Christianity had but a weak grip on men's souls whatever their rank in society. In addition, the Church was being destroyed from within by furious hatreds which were given open expression of a character that it is impossible for us to imagine since the Reformation. . . . Injuries, assaults, and bloodshed between clerks were not rare. The Church frequently became involved in violent conflicts with the bourgeoisie of the towns and ill treated its serfs. Tonsured vagabonds and criminals were numerous. . . . In the towns, disorder was complicated by the grave dissensions arising between rich and poor. The greater burgesses monopolized municipal office, governed the free towns to their own advantages, and oppressed the lower order until their egotism stimulated revolt. . . .[1]

Certainly the Gothic cathedral is related to an historical situation, but it is not the spontaneous and unreflected-upon expression of a pervasive spirit of Christian piety that Augustus Pugin fancied it was. We must try to discover if we can the specific circumstances in which specific inventions were made and the basis of the subsequent popularity of those inventions in certain places and among certain classes of the society. Unfortunately, we know little about the lives and thoughts of most of the people who were involved in the creation of Gothic art. We do not even know their names; but that is not at all to say that they were anonymous.

The style was invented in the second quarter of the twelfth century in the region of Paris—that is, in the Royal Domain of the Capetian kings of France. The situation to which it addressed itself was similar to the one we discussed in connection with the design of the Cathedral of Worms: it involved a balance of power among four elements in the make-up of French society at the time—the king and his court, the church, the feudal nobility, and the rising bourgeoisie. At the beginning of the twelfth century relations among these factions were frequently as strained and as hostile as was the case in Germany. Consider, for instance, Arthur Kingsley Porter's account of the founding of the commune of Laon.

In 1111 the town of Laon rose against its bishop. Isolated on their steep rock the inhabitants of this city lived amid constant civil war and class hatred; noble held bourgeois for ransom, bourgeois robbed and pillaged peasant. The king himself was not safe in this strange town. Gaudri, bishop of Laon, was blessed with a character almost as pleasant as that of his people. He treated his townsmen as serfs, thought only of war and hunting, and always appeared in public followed by a negro slave who was his official executioner. To dispose of a baron who annoyed him this Christian prelate did not hesitate to have him assassinated in a church.

Profiting by the absence of Gaudri in England the bourgeois bought from the clergy and nobles the privilege of forming a corporation. When the bishop returned and learned of this transaction, he was furious; but he was appeased by a large sum of money, and even swore to protect the commune. Louis VI, also well paid, confirmed the charter (1111).

The following year the King happened to come to Laon, and Gaudri planned to improve the opportunity afforded by his presence to destroy the commune. The bourgeois discovered the plot, and offered Louis 400 pounds to remain faithful to his promise; but the bishop offered him 700 to break it. The last bid being the higher the commune was abolished. At this, the popular indignation not unnaturally ran high. The king found it prudent to slip out of the city before daybreak. At sunrise bands of bourgeois armed with swords and axes rushed upon the episcopal palace, and massacred all within. A serf knocked out the brains of the bishop by a blow of his ax. Then the tumult extended, the houses of nobles and clergy were attacked, and the inmates escaped only by disguising themselves and taking flight. Fire and pillage followed; the cathedral church was burned to the ground.

The murder of a bishop could not be left unavenged. The royal army accordingly marched against the revolted city, and took it by storm. Then it was the turn of the nobles and clergy to massacre the bourgeois. Finally the peasants of the neighborhood swarmed into the ruined town, and pillaged the deserted houses. The commune was wiped out in blood (1114). Sixteen years later, however, it was reestablished. Political circumstances had forced the King and the Church to grant municipal government to the bourgeois. . . .

The bourgeois of Amiens rose in revolt about the same time (1113). Their commune was established only after four years of bitter warfare, although the bishop backed the townsmen against the count. Louis VI at last turned the balance in favor of the bourgeois.[2]

The first step toward the development of the Gothic was taken at this point, when the king and certain bishops in the Royal Domain decided to support the demands of the burghers against the feudal aristocracy, both secular and monastic. Though this new alignment was never unambiguous or free of dissension, the Gothic flourished while it lasted. We even know with reasonable certainty who was responsible for the new policy: it was probably the work of the Abbot Suger (ca. 1081-1151), whose name is inextricably linked with the origins of Gothic architecture.

Suger was of humble birth. As a young boy he entered the school of the Abbey of S. Denis, near Paris—the royal abbey, of which Carolingians and Capetians had been honorary abbots, where Pepin had been crowned, and where many kings and queens were buried. There he formed a close friendship with a fellow student of his own age, the future King Louis VI (the Fat). In 1122 Suger was made abbot of the monastery, which, though it was one of the richest establishments in France, was corrupt and dilapidated. He set to work to reform its life and to rebuild its church from the ground up. Though the building he erected was largely demolished in the following century to make way for a still finer one, there is reason to believe that it was the first

Gothic church. He himself was to speak of it in terms which suggest that he thought it the embodiment of a mystical and transcendent religious faith, a place where he was "lifted in a mystic manner" from the material world to an immaterial realm of radiant splendor. Yet Suger was scarcely a mystic. He was a political administrator of extraordinary sagacity, an intimate adviser to both Louis VI and Louis VII. In fact, while the latter was absent on crusade in the 1140s, Suger was regent of France. He was the king's man.

Now the Capetian kings, like their Ottonian kinsmen, had long dreamed of uniting their feudalized kingdom and of establishing a monarchy that could be compared with Charlemagne's. Today it is hard for us to grasp the extent to which feudal institutions had divided the country. Not only were there the great duchies and counties, presided over by lords whose power sometimes exceeded that of the king; the entire countryside was divided and subdivided, parceled out among hundreds of petty feudatories. Even the cities were formed by the consolidation of feudal holdings, which nevertheless remained under the control of aristocratic families. Paris was composed of at least thirty-four such districts, Tours of thirty-one, other cities of comparable numbers. In each urban district justice was administered by the controlling family; and since in the Middle Ages to judge was to govern, this meant that the government was not really in the king's hands in Paris itself, to say nothing of the remote duchies. There had been a time, during the Norman invasions, when those innumerable lordlings had served a necessary function as military guardians; but by the twelfth century, when the towns had grown large and prosperous, they were of little use to anyone, though they continued to exact tolls and duties and taxes of every variety from the merchants within their districts and from traders traversing their roads or using their bridges. It was in order to free themselves from these burdensome vestiges of feudalism that the burghers fought for, or purchased, the right to organize self-governing communes.

As Suger well knew, the Ottonian emperors had failed in their attempt at unification because they had lost the support of the church. Facing a situation similar to theirs, the abbot evidently perceived that though there was little chance of subjugating the great dukes, the power of the king would exceed that of any of them if the secular church and the rich burghers were on his side. He must have come to recognize that the critical factor in the political equation at that moment was the episcopate; for the bishops' loyalties were essentially divided. As landlords they had a stake in the agrarian establishment that included also the monastic church and the feudal nobility, and as princes of the church they owed allegiance to the pope in Rome. Yet the monasteries had by then become so powerful that they were claiming exemption from episcopal authority and demanding the right to be answerable directly to the pope. Monks were being elected to the papacy, and the influence of the Abbot of Cluny in the councils of the church was probably second only to that of the pope himself. Gregory VII, Urban II, and Paschal II were all Cluniac monks, while Innocent II and Eugenius III owed their elevation to Clairvaux and St. Bernard. Plainly the power of the monks had been gained at the bishops' expense. As a result, the latter were inclined to ally themselves with the king rather than with Rome. Here lay the roots of the Gallicanism which was to play an important part in welding together the modern French nation.

Every episcopal diocese was known by the name of a city; every bishop had his palace in a town, over which he exercised regulatory authority in various ways. During the eleventh century the bishops had often used their power in order to impose restrictions upon the growing class of merchants, with whom they, as landed lords, had little sympathy. But the bishop who held fast to a feudal conception of his prerogatives was threatened with the fate of the Bishop of Laon. Moreover, the townsmen of the twelfth century were increasingly inclined toward a skeptical secularism or else toward pietistic and proto-Protestant heresies such as those of Peter of Bruys and of Peter Waldo.

Plainly a policy was needed that would restore the preeminence of the episcopate within the church, that would strengthen the hand of the king against the separatist tendencies of the aristocracy, that would reaffirm the sacred and priestly nature of kingship, and that would win the favor of the rebellious burghers. Thanks to Suger, we suppose, that policy began to take shape in the 1120s and '30s. Its main emphasis was upon gaining a consensus, upon achieving unity and agreement, upon allaying the social and spiritual disturbances of the "renaissance of the twelfth century." In the jargon of our own day we might say that what was called for was a new image, both of the monarchy and of the episcopacy.

A new image but not a revolution; the policy was essentially one of institutional stabilization. For this reason, nothing was more important to its realization than the art of architecture. The word "Gothic" can scarcely be separated in our minds from the word "cathedral." The latter word is derived, of course, from the Latin *cathedra,* which for the republican Romans had designated simply a comfortable armchair. In the Middle Ages the word meant "throne"; a cathedral church is one that houses the throne of a bishop, whose hierarchical rank was equivalent to that of a duke. Although the great cathedrals of the twelfth and thirteenth centuries were designed to be as attractive as possible, to present the church in the best possible light, and to stand for an ideal of urban unity in the face of feudal divisiveness, they also declared unmistakably the absolute primacy of the church and its bishop in the life of the city.

Because of their titanic size—they were the largest single buildings that had been erected since the construction of the pyramids—it was popularly believed a century ago that they had been created by the sacrifices and collaboration of the entire town. Much was made then of the Cult of the Carts, a kind of penance that originated at Chartres before the middle of the twelfth century and that led the citizens of that city, and of others in northwestern France, to harness themselves to heavy carts in order to haul from a distance the stone and other materials that were needed for the erection of churches. Today we are not so sure just what to make of the phenomenon. No doubt it was a

Figure 45. View of Cathedral of Amiens, 1220-1269. (Courtesy of Photographie Giraudon, Paris.)

F-17

time when many people could be aroused to passionately enthusiastic action (witness the response to Peter the Hermit's preaching of the First Crusade), for the reason, perhaps, that the immanence of the sacred in objects, persons, and events seemed far more obvious then than it does to us today. Penance, however, is a sacrament of the church, and deeds performed for the expiation of sin are prescribed by the sinner's confessor. There is some reason to believe that the in-itiative, in the matter of the carts, lay with the clergy. The popular fervor that attended the episode was unquestionably sincere, but it was short-lived; it could not be maintained over the long periods of time that cathedral building required.

In times of fervor and of municipal prosperity the citizens probably made substantial contributions toward defraying the staggering expenses involved in the enterprise. Yet we must keep it in mind that the build-ings were in large part paid for by the bishops themselves, with income derived from their extensive lands and from the various taxes they levied on commerce. While the cathedrals were constructed by wage-earning craftsmen and were designed to appeal to the burgher's pride of city and to his taste for fine and costly craftsmanship, the financial burden involved was ultimately borne, in the main, by the grossly exploited peasantry.

The cathedrals affirm the sacral nature of monarchy and the indis-soluble alliance of church and state. Nowhere can the union of the secular with the ecclesiastical be expounded more cogently than in the handling of the doorways of a church. In Romanesque architecture, as we have seen, the entrance was often treated as a point of maximal tension or ambivalence. The Gothic period may well be said to have begun with the invention of a new kind of doorway.

When Suger acceded to the abbacy of St. Denis in 1122 and turned his attention to improving the abbey church, what struck him first was the narrowness and the inadequacy of its portals; whereupon he had designed for his new church a broad façade with spacious and inviting entrances, the first doors in the new manner that came to be called Gothic. In their embrasures stood sculptured figures which, because they were destroyed during the Revolution, are known to us only in old drawings. Most of the statues represented the royal ancestors of Christ, who are enumerated by both Matthew and Luke. Interspersed among these kings and queens were images of Old Testament priests and prophets. Not only did the portals declare the Biblical basis of the condominium of king and clergy; they so presented the idea as to make it seem that those figures of archetypal royalty formed of themselves a numerous congregation that stood handsomely and attractively within

the portals of the church. The kingly figures of Byzantine and Romanesque art are typically seated upon thrones, in images that are normally
located in distant or lofty regions of the church building. Suger's image
of royalty is *popular* in form, location, grouping, and address.

Another such portal, which was probably completed before Suger's
death in 1151, has fortunately come down to us almost intact. Early in
the 1140s the abbot's good friend Geoffroy, Bishop of Chartres, was
inspired to begin work on a new façade for his Romanesque cathedral.
Between two massive towers that are somewhat different from one another in design,[3] there is enframed a markedly vertical panel that contains an enormous circular window filled with an intricate pattern of
lesser circles; three great lancet windows in which the earliest stained
glass in the building is to be found; and, below these, the celebrated

F-18

Figure 46. Façade, Cathedral of
Chartres, ca. 1145 et ff. (Cour-
tesy of Archives photographiques,
Paris.)

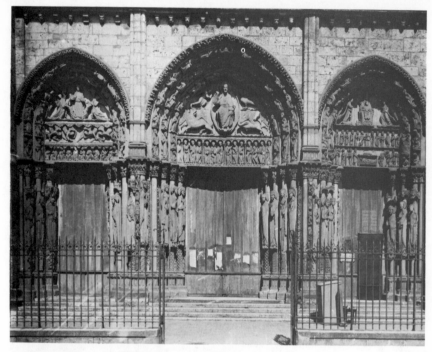

Figure 47. Royal Portals, Cathedral of Chartres, *ca.* 1145. (Courtesy of Archives photographiques, Paris.)

Chartres   F-19

Royal Portals (Fig. 47), whose decorative scheme includes three sculptured tympana, about seventy-five archivolt figures, a frieze of nativity and passion scenes covering the capitals of the engaged columns, and, against the columns themselves, nineteen (originally twenty-two) larger-than-life-sized statues of the royal ancestors and prophets, which again declare the elegance and amiability of an institutional aristocracy.

Since each figure is attached to a column, the mode of grouping is unmistakably associated with the very structure of the church itself. In some ways these columnar statues are analogous to the caryatids of ancient Greece; but whereas the latter figures constitute the structure— are themselves the working members of the larger whole—the medieval images are conformed to an order of things which is immeasurably larger than they are and has a self-sufficient existence apart from them. The true caryatid is not to be found in medieval architecture. Romanesque and Gothic buildings alike defend a theory of the state and church that attributes to those institutions an absolute reality and a structure-

giving power that do not find their source in the citizen-members themselves. But where the Romanesque statue is, more often than not, con-
fined within an architectural frame, the portal figures of the Gothic
cathedrals are not separated from one another by the architecture but
seem, instead, to form a warmly human group and to occupy the portal
space in much the same way as do the members of the congregation
who contemplate them from the pavement below.

One of the evident concerns of the Gothic artist, early and late,
was to achieve an ideal amalgamation of the courtly with the liturgical.
He speaks in defense of the sacramental and sacerdotal aspects of institutional practice that were then being attacked by heretics such as
the Petrobrusians and the Henricians. Though the Royal Portals as a
whole, and indeed the entire cathedral, are involved in that defense,
the message is conveyed most incisively, as Katzenellenbogen has demonstrated, in the tympanum, archivolts, and lintel of the right-hand
portal of the west façade (Fig. 48). In the tympanum we see the

Figure 48. South tympanum, west façade, Cathedral of Chartres, ca.
1145. (Courtesy of Archives photographiques, Paris.)

F-20

Chartres

Virgin and Child regally enthroned between angels. The Nativity scenes below are handled in such a way as to stress the Eucharistic or sacramental aspect of the Incarnation; the anecdotal liveliness with which the Romanesque artist had commonly represented such scenes gives way here to a "static and diagrammatic system." In the *Presentation in the Temple* the Child is placed directly upon the altar, while each of the thirteen figures in the scene is carefully centered beneath a little arch. Their arrangement is as stately as that of the great piers of the nave arcade inside the church. In the *Nativity* at the bottom level the Virgin's bed becomes an altar also, on top of which the Child is again placed as a living sacrifice. In the archivolts at either side of these scenes are figures representing the seven liberal arts—a premonitory indication, perhaps, of the critically important role that was to be played by the learned schoolmen of the period (and was already being played by the School of Chartres) in the defense of ecclesiastical orthodoxy.

The sculptural style of the west façade is still archaic. The embrasure figures resemble in several ways (*e.g.*, in their frontality, in the

Chartres

F-21

Figure 49. Embrasure figures, west façade, Cathedral of Chartres, ca. 1145. (Courtesy of Archives photographiques, Paris.)

suggestion about their mouths of an "archaic smile," in the rendering
of drapery in a succession of finely pleated parallel folds) the so-called
Acropolis Maidens that were made in Athens around 520 B.C. Moreover,
the kings and queens were probably painted, as were the Maidens.
Unlike the Greek figures, however, they are strikingly attenuated, to
such an extent that several of the female figures are approximately ten
heads high. That is to say, the total height of the figure is about ten
times that of the head, in contrast to a biological norm of about six
and a half times. Greatly elongated figures are to be found in the Romanesque art of the preceding generation, as in the tympanum at
Autun (Fig. 33), but the meaning of the usage has now changed:
whereas at Autun the attenuation of some figures and the compression
of others contribute to an over-all appearance of writhing agitation, at
Chartres elongation denotes aristocracy—for of course everyone knows
that bluebloods are tall and slender, with narrow shoulders and small
hands and feet, and that only peasants have large heads and squat,
stocky bodies.

In 1194 the old Romanesque church behind Geoffroy's façade was
destroyed, along with much of the town, by a disastrous fire. After an
initial feeling of dismay, the citizens had the happy thought that the
fire had occurred because the Virgin, whose special favor toward Chartres they traced back to pre-Christian times, wanted the city to have
a larger and finer church, equal or superior to the one that was then
being constructed in her honor in Paris. The old façade was left standing, since it had not been damaged, and behind it there was erected a
modern church (the word *modern* was used then, too) that was some
440 feet long and whose vaults reached a height of more than 120 feet
above the floor. The structural system that is typical of all the French
Gothic cathedrals (Fig. 50) is now fully developed: ribbed vaults are
carried on comparatively slender supporting members (Fig. 51) and
are braced against collapse by the dead weight of great piers of masonry
that are placed at right angles to the outer edge of the main floor area
of the church and are joined to the vaults by "flying" buttresses—that
is, by stone bars which are held up by segmental arches.

Two generations ago the system was regarded as the principal expressive feature, the chief embodiment of the meaning, of the Gothic
church. As a constructional invention it is admirably ingenious; but
since one can never see both the outside and the inside of the church
at the same time, its constructivist logic is not visibly and affectingly
apparent in the architectural forms. However, the invention does make
possible the towering height of the Gothic interior; it promotes the
structural skeletonization which enables the builder to devote the great-

Chartres

F-22

Figure 50. Lateral section, Cathedral of Chartres, 1194 *et ff.* (From: Dehio und Bezold, *Die kirchliche Baukunst des Abendlandes*, Stuttgart, 1884-1901.)

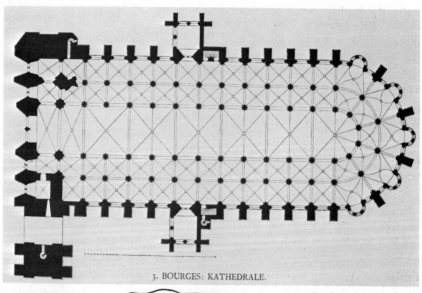

3. BOURGES: KATHEDRALE.

Figure 51. Plan, Cathedral of Bourges, 1190-1275. (From Dehio & Bezold.)

F-23

er part of the wall area to a sumptuous display of stained glass; and
it produces an exterior structure which, because of its profusion of
small, projecting, fragile, perforated elements, seems feminine and lux-
urious in comparison with the fortress-like stolidity of the typical Romanesque exterior.

This is not to say, of course, that the church had ceased to be militant: four Crusades were launched against the Holy Land during the
thirteenth century, while between 1208 and 1229 many of the French
bishops actually led military forces in the ruthless and exterminatory
campaign that was conducted, partly for political reasons, against the
Albigensian heretics in Languedoc. Certainly the Gothic cathedral speaks
persuasively of unity, of the collaboration of innumerable members (there
are some 1,800 sculptured figures on the exterior of the Cathedral of
Chartres, for instance) in something that is exalting and exciting; but
the building should not be taken as evidence of a radical change in
the conduct of medieval Christians.

The cavernous new doorways of the transepts at Chartres were
erected some sixty or seventy years after the completion of the Royal
Portals of the old façade. As had happened in Greece between 520 and
460 B.C., it was during this period of time that the sculptor laid aside
the archaic conventions of his immediate forebears and developed a
style of the kind we are accustomed to calling classical. To pass from
the queens of the west façade to the Ste. Modeste (Fig. 52) of the
north transept is like going from the Acropolis Maidens to the caryatids
of the Erechtheum. Her context is still wholly architectural (though
more varied and irregular than had been the case on the façade), and
the sculptor's concern is still with defining the ideal of the saintly gen-
tlelady rather than with specifying the character or identity of a person.
Yet the figure seems now to turn easily from left to right, and the
drapery, which is gathered at the waist to reveal something of the
structure of the body, falls loosely from the shoulders and hips and
breaks into many soft folds around the feet. The idea of aristocracy
is now expressed in terms of gesture, stance, demeanour, not by arbi-
trary attenuation; the figure is six and a half heads high.

Something of the direction of the development of figural art in
the following decades, or even in the next two hundred years, can be
descried in the sculptures of the central portal of a façade of the Cathedral of Rheims (Fig. 53). The two pairs of figures on the right-hand
embrasure, which were probably carved in the middle years of the
thirteenth century, represent the Annunciation and the Visitation, while
the four figures of the left embrasure are devoted to the Presentation

Chartres

Figure 52. *Ste. Modeste. North transept portal, Cathedral of Chartres. (Photo by author.)*   *P-24*

in the Temple. The central position that is here accorded the Nativity scenes is itself indicative of the increasing importance of a narrational, as opposed to an iconic or hieratic, religious imagery. Instead of portraying kings and queens who are united by their membership in a privileged class, these figures show the bringing of good news, the meeting of two expectant mothers, and the handing of a baby into the hands of an old priest. All these are familiar human actions and relationships of a kind that lead us directly toward the subject matter of Renaissance painting.

In style, moreover, these are the most varied of all Gothic portal figures. One may explain the stylistic disparities by observing that some of the figures were made by masters who had been trained at Chartres and at Amiens before coming to Rheims, where work was still in progress after those other cathedrals had been finished. That was undoubtedly the case: the figure of the Virgin in the Rheims *Annunciation* is striking-

ly similar to figures in the right portal at Amiens, while the prophets
in the right portal at Rheims are plainly akin to the prophets of the
north transept at Chartres. There is a little evidence, furthermore, in
favor of Reinhardt's contention that some of the statues at Rheims were
made for a façade that was planned by Jean d'Orbais in the 1220s and
were later incorporated, somewhat awkwardly, in the design that was
carried out some years later. Yet it would scarcely have been possible
for the various artists who came together at Rheims to ignore their
differences of manner. One can speak of a "workshop style" at Chartres
and at Amiens; but when Reinhardt invents "*l'atelier des Vierges*" and
"*l'atelier de Simeon et de David*" he is using the word "shop" where
he should be saying "master." What one sees emerging at Rheims is an
individualized practice that is clearly related to the contemporaneous
appearance in Italy of the first artists who are known to us both by
name and by virtue of their stylistic originality—artists such as Bona-
ventura Berlinghieri, Nicola Pisano, and Jacopo Torriti.

In the Virgin of the *Annunciation* the artist from Amiens chose to
carve a simple, sedate, and rather grave figure that was designed to

Figure 53. *Annunciation* and *Visitation*. Central portal, west façade,
Cathedral of Rheims, *ca.* 1240. (Courtesy of Archives photographiques,
Paris.)

F-25   Rheims

appeal, we should imagine, to the kind of bourgeois taste that was later attracted by the works of Giotto in Florence and of the Lorenzetti brothers in Siena. The angel beside her, on the other hand, exhibits a mincing elegance and courtly attenuation that are addressed rather, one might say, to the "Ghibelline" taste that was predominant in the secular scriptoria of Paris in the mid thirteenth century and that found expression later in the paintings of Simone Martini and of Jean Pucelle and, still later, in those of the International Style.

Most interesting of all are the statues of Mary and Elizabeth in the *Visitation* group, for they were unquestionably inspired by works of Roman sculpture—though by what specific works, in what medium and of what size, we do not know. We come face to face here with a difficult problem about which a great deal has been written during the past century: that of the survival and revival of the forms of Graeco-Roman art in the Middle Ages.[4] All medieval images of the human body lie within a tradition that reaches back to ancient Rome. That tradition underwent radical changes, as we have seen, but it was never entirely broken. One must also remember, however, that not only were many works of Roman sculpture visible in medieval Europe, but they were sometimes admired as aesthetic objects, even though it was recognized that they were incommensurable with the attitudes of the medieval church. At least one of the figurated capitals by Gislebertus of Autun is clearly based on an ancient source, whose shapes the Romanesque artist undoubtedly found attractive. Yet he borrows from antiquity somewhat as Picasso does: he adapts a composition to his own uses, but he rejects the spirit in which it was originally conceived. From the mid twelfth century onward, we find evidence (*e.g.*, in the enamels of Nicholas of Verdun) of a growing understanding or genuine fellow feeling between the medieval townsman-artist and his ancient predecessor. We can sense something of the excitement the *Visitation* sculptor must have experienced as he tried, however awkwardly, to lay hold again upon an image of the poised, purposeful, self-conscious, responsible human being as it had been revealed to him in some Roman fragment that he was at last beginning to *see*.

Not that the *Visitation* figures are more "realistic" than the others: they seem ungainly and badly proportioned in comparison with the Virgin of the *Annunciation* group, whose sculptor was masterfully in control of his ideas and materials. What matters is that under the clinging drapery of Elizabeth one detects the rudiments of a *contrapposto* figure, standing on its own feet and adjusting its weight within a gravitational field. The sculptor had not looked carefully at his Roman model, nor had he tested or experimented with the stance the model revealed to him. Recognizing that the pose involved a straight leg and a bent leg, a high shoulder and a low shoulder, he reasoned himself into the notion that the low shoulder should be over the bent leg, the high shoulder over the straight one—though as any Greek sculptor could have told him, or as he could have discovered for himself by looking at the apprentice who was standing idly before his work across the shop, it is the other way around. Nevertheless, for all his ineptitude the *Visitation* master had something to say that would eventually make the architectonic schema of the Gothic façade untenable—though its diagrammatic program would continue to find defenders for another two hundred and fifty years or more.

Perhaps it was recognized that he had gone too far, for the classicizing tendency of the first half of the thirteenth century is virtually extinguished in the second half, to be supplanted by a mannered style of exaggerated courtliness and curvilinearity that stresses the aristocratic element in Gothic art at the expense of its burgherly aspect. The ideas that had found expression among the townsmen of the Royal Domain were passed, partly by way of the Hohenstaufen kingdom in southern Italy, to the North Italian city-states. The spiritual if not the lineal descendants of the *Visitation* figures at Rheims are to be found in Giotto's Arena Chapel.

The classic example of the full-blown Gothic façade is that of the Cathedral of Amiens (Fig. 54). With its many projections and perforations, its lavish display of ornament, its cavernous portals inhabited by a multitudinous assembly of saints and angels, all presided over by the stately, sacerdotal figure of the *Beau Dieu* (Fig. 55) on the central trumeau, it strikes a perfect balance between grandeur and grace, stability and animation, rectitude and pomp. Like the atrium of the fourth-century church, the Gothic portal is a preparatory space; but what it affirms is not the separation of the church from the world but rather the possibility of an ideal and harmonious union between the two—between the Christian's life in the world and his membership within an order of things that both embraces and transcends that life. By the time one reaches the doors of the church, one is already encompassed by the building and by its patterns of congregation and communion.

Certainly the aspect of the cathedral that most impresses us today is its interior. To walk for the first time beneath the towering vaults and among the huge piers of Amiens or Rheims or Chartres is probably the most exciting experience that the art of architecture has to offer us. No other kind of building affords the observer such a variety of astonishing perspectives, such rich effects of radiance and of shadowy mystery. And yet, oddly enough, we do not know what importance the

Amiens
← F-26

Figure 54. Façade, Cathedral of Amiens, 1220-1269. (Courtesy of Archives photographiques, Paris.)

F-27 *Amiens* →

Figure 55. *Le Beau Dieu*, central trumeau, west façade, Cathedral of Amiens, *ca.* 1240. (Courtesy of Archives photographiques, Paris.)

Figure 56. Interior, Cathedral of Amiens, 1220-1269. (Courtesy of Archives photographiques, Paris.)

F-28

builders of the cathedrals attached to such experiences. We value them because we are very much preoccupied, as men have been increasingly for the past six hundred years, with the qualitative existence of the single person in his privacy—witness the conceptions of purpose, value, and style that underly all twentieth-century painting. There is reason to believe, however, that the medieval architect was less interested in manipulating the psychological responses of the worshiper than in erecting a suitable Palace of the Queen of Heaven. That is to say, the validity of the building lay in its relationship to the Virgin and to the unshakable reality of the institutions of church, monarchy, and city, rather than in its power to arouse a response in a self-centered observer.

For one thing, there is no element of perspective vista in thirteenth-century painting. When the illuminator of the Psalter of St. Louis (Fig. 57) employs the Gothic cathedral as an ideal frame for a series of Old Testament illustrations, he chooses its exterior rather than its interior aspect; there is no connection whatever between the picture spaces, such as they are, and the architectural spaces of the building itself. He conceives of the building as an object still, not as a field of personal experience. When finally it is so conceived, by Van Eyck and Van der Weyden in the fifteenth century, the townsman's enthusiasm for erecting colossal cathedrals is dead.

Another bit of evidence is to be found, perhaps, in the stained glass windows, which are the chief glory of the cathedral interior. Throughout the Middle Ages the decoration of the church with narrative imagery was justified (against recurrent charges of idolatry) on the ground that it enabled the illiterate poor to read in pictures what

Figure 57. *Joshua Bidding the Sun Stand Still.* Psalter of St. Louis (B. N. lat. 10525), *ca.* 1260. (By permission of Bibliothèque nationale, Paris.)

they could not read in books. That the stained glass windows were ever used for instructional or didactic purposes, however, seems highly improbable. The little medallion scenes in the typical thirteenth-century window are so small as to be scarcely discernible from the floor below. Unlike the lively narrational images of Romanesque art, they are submerged within the total convention of the palatial cathedral and quite lack the pictorial incisiveness of both earlier and later depictions. To a great extent they are overwhelmed by the medium itself. The sheer visual splendor of a high Gothic window, with its thousands upon thousands of chips of predominantly red, blue, yellow, and white glass, is such that we cannot bring ourselves to scrutinize carefully or to take seriously the little nondescript representations that are embedded in its sumptuously ornate patterns. It is probably fair to say that no significant invention in the art of painting was made by stained glass workers. Their art was rather employed, it would seem, to hold back a development of the human imagination that would lead inevitably to the imagery of Masaccio and Van Eyck—and to the undoing of both the cosmology and the institutional balance of power which the cathedral was built to defend.

Since the appearance of Gothic architecture coincided with the rise of commercial cities throughout Western Europe, and since the style was designed especially to appeal to the tastes and to engage the sympathies of the newly prosperous bourgeoisie, it is not surprising that it should have spread rapidly into every corner of the Catholic world. But since other regions were faced with social and institutional situations that were different from the one that had given rise to the French cathedral, many local variants of the style were devised, among which the only common denominator is the use of the pointed arch and the ribbed vault. Occasionally, as in the Cathedral of Cologne and in London's Westminster Abbey, the French example is followed rather closely—though in those cases, too, there are significant departures.

In France, as we have seen, the Gothic cathedral represented, among other things, an ambitious assertion of episcopal primacy in the face of what must have seemed to the bishops a usurpation of power by the monastic church—an institution that was increasingly despised by the burghers, as well. In England, on the other hand, the distinction between the secular and the regular (or monastic) church was much less clearly drawn. Christianity had been reintroduced into Britain in the 590s by a Benedictine monk, St. Augustine, and the church he formed by joining forces with the Celtic foundations was monastic in orientation from the beginning. Time and again, after the disruptions of Danish and Norman invasion, it was restored by monastic reformers. Lanfranc, William's Archbishop of Canterbury, reorganized many of the major cathedral establishments as cathedral-priories, thereby placing their administration in the hands of a monastic or quasi-monastic chapter; whereafter it was normal for the English cathedral to be adjoined by a cloister, a chapter house, dormitories, refectories, and other conventual buildings. Neither the abbots nor the bishops of England were inclined toward allying themselves with town or crown. Open hostility between church and laity persisted throughout the Gothic era, so that when Henry VIII, after severing ties with Rome, abolished the monasteries and confiscated their property, he had the support of the Parliament and, by and large, of the people.

In view of this situation, it is not surprising to find that English Gothic architecture is extremely conservative. The long, low, angular silhouette of the Romanesque church is generally preserved, its major accent being provided by the lantern tower over the crossing rather than by a grandiose western façade. By holding down the height of his vaulted ceilings, which are about half as high as those of the French cathedrals, the English architect could reduce or eliminate the need for elaborate exterior buttressing and so could retain the blocklike massing and the external austerity of the architecture of the twelfth century. His façades (Fig. 58) are like flattened screens; they are less sculpturesque in form and less generously decorated with sculpture than is the case in France. When sculpture is used, as at Wells and Salisbury, it is distributed over the façade, after the manner of the Angevin Romanesque (cf. Cathedral of Angoulême); the figures are not gathered into congregational groupings, nor do they share architectural spaces with the entering worshiper. (In fact, the small western doors of the cathedral were rarely used. The English church is normally entered by way of a side porch.)

One of the distinctive peculiarities of the English cathedral is its rectangular east end, in contrast to the radial chevet of most continental churches. Historians have suggested various practical considerations that may have had some bearing on the popularity of the usage, but in point of fact, what was done in an English church could have been done quite as well in a French one. The usage has been attributed to Cistercian influence; but though the flat-ended plan was favored by the Cistercians, there is no self-evident reason why their influence should have been stronger in England than elsewhere. It is only when we consider the character of the English church as a whole that we can make sense of

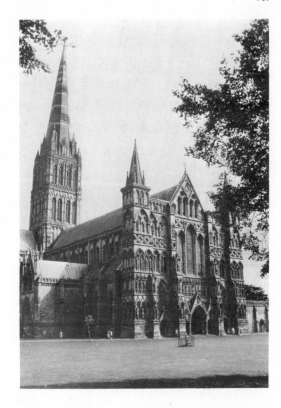

E-4

Figure 58. Façade, Cathedral of Salisbury, 1220-1258. (Photo by author.)

the squared end; for it is closely bound up with another distinguishing feature of the building—namely, its greatly extended choir, the length of which usually approaches and sometimes equals or exceeds that of the nave. Those of a functionalist turn of mind have argued that the additional space was needed because of the large size of the cathedral chapter and because of its need for additional altars for its many priests. The evidence does not bear out such contentions. The clergy were not so numerous as to require half of a vast cathedral for themselves.

One need only glance at an English plan, such as that of the Cathedral of York (one of the least monasticized of the major foundations), in order to see that the church consists essentially of two naves rather than of nave and apse. Between the two, at the crossing, there was customarily erected a rood screen or organ screen that clearly separated the one from the other. Two sets of services were commonly conducted in the church: one for the clergy in the choir, another for the laity in the nave.

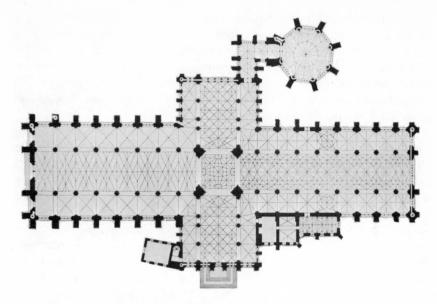

Figure 59. Plan, Cathedral of York, 1261. (From Dehio & Bezold.)

E-5

From earliest times the rectangular hall had been the gathering place of the *ecclesia*, or Christian assembly, which in the beginning was presided over, it would seem, only by the presbyters or elders of the group. Later, whén there had come into being a fully professional clergy that was endowed with a measure of magisterial authority, an elevated apsidal space was provided in order to make a distinction between the priesthood and the laity within the now well-established institution of the church. With the rapid development of cenobitic monasticism after the fall of Rome, however, there appeared a second Christian community, all of whose members were ordained priests. The orders constituted an increasingly separate "religious" church that had its own self-sufficient societies operating side by side in the world with those of the "secular" Christians.

In the mid twelfth century the French bishops had successfully challenged the pretensions of that second community, whose wealth and power were disproportionately great in relation to the size of its membership. In England, on the other hand, the secular clergy aligned themselves with their monastic brethren and stressed the distinction between the religious community and the lay community—wherefore the two naves. It is interesting to compare this institutional duality with the one that had developed in Charlemagne's time. In that earlier case there was produced a church building with a single nave and two apses; in the latter, two naves but no apse. In the one it was asserted, so to speak, that there was a single community that was oriented in two directions; in the other, that the church consisted of two separate but equal communities. By contrast, nave and apse are more harmoniously merged with one another in the French Gothic cathedral than in any other kind of church ever invented (cf. Fig. 51).

In Italy the Roman tradition of urban living did not die out during the Dark Ages as it did in Gaul and Britain. Although the great Italian cities of antiquity shrank to small size, they remained centers of political power at all times; for while there was a land-holding aristocracy, it had been customary since the early days of the Roman Republic for the senatorial gentry to reside in cities and to participate in the affairs of city government rather than to sequester themselves in country strongholds. On the other hand, Italy had no king, no single ruler with the zeal for unification that motivated the Ottonians, the Capetians, and the Plantagenets. It follows, therefore, that the situation out of which the Gothic style developed in France and that promoted its dissemination throughout the monarchical lands of Germany, England, and Spain, simply did not exist in Italy, which was dominated by strong city-states already in the eleventh century.

But since the elegant and extravagant Gothic art of France had been designed to appeal to the bourgeoisie, certain limited aspects of that art did enjoy a brief and belated popularity among the Italian townsmen. Most of the great Gothic churches of that country were begun toward the very end of the thirteenth century, by which time the passion for cathedral building was rapidly declining in the North. Indeed, the taste for the Gothic was scarcely more than a passing fad in Italy.

The burghers of Florence and Bologna, Venice and Milan, Siena and Orvieto, were duly impressed by, and perhaps a bit envious of, the gigantic cathedral churches of the French towns. Not to be outdone, they saw to it that their own cities were provided with Gothic churches of comparable size. In Italy, however, the introduction of the new style was not attended by an important change of policy on the part of the ruling classes, nor by the propagation of a radically new image of institutional authority. The Italians were less inclined to look back to an idealized and legendary Charlemagne than to the example of Rome— as the Pisans were doing already in the mid eleventh century, as we have seen. The Italian Gothic church typically has none of the lacy fragility of the French palaces of the Queen of Heaven; in their massiveness and grandeur they remind us rather of the great basilican halls

Figure 60. Interior, Cathedral of Florence, 1296 *et ff.* (Courtesy of Dr. Franz Stoedtner, Düsseldorf.)

of ancient Rome. Their exterior walls are not hidden behind a proliferation of flying buttresses, pinnacles, and gargoyles, their doorways are not decorated with figures of aristocratic saints, their interior structure is not elaborately membered. They speak of unity, but in terms that would have been more readily understandable to Masaccio and Donatello than to the painter of the Psalter of St. Louis. In a number of cases, as at Siena and Orvieto, the architect made only marginal and decorative use of the pointed arch and clung instead to the rounded form of the Romanesque style that would lead so easily and directly into the Renaissance classicism of Brunelleschi.

It is in Italy and Flanders—the two regions that would produce the most distinguished painting of the early Renaissance—that we find the earliest examples of the Gothic town hall. Virtually all such buildings, as in Bruges and Siena, possess clock towers that rise as high as the pinnacle of the cathedral's spire or bell tower. In every case they are aggressive assertions of the city's freedom from that ecclesiastical and episcopal domination that the Gothic style had originally been

Figure 61. Interior, Cathedral of Orvieto, 1290-1310. (Courtesy of Dr. Franz Stoedtner, Düsseldorf.)

devised to defend. It is in one of the handsomest of these, the Palazzo Pubblico of Siena, that we discover those first great works of secular imagery—the *Guidoriccio* fresco by Simone Martini (1328) and the panoramic vistas of city and countryside in Ambrogio Lorenzetti's *Good Government* frescoes (*ca.* 1340)—with the appearance of which we may say that we have unquestionably passed beyond the realm of medieval art, with its predilection for flattened diagrams and structural schemata, and into that of the Renaissance.

FOOTNOTES

[1]Petit-Dutaillis, Charles E., *The Feudal Monarchy in France and England from the Tenth to the Thirteenth Century.* (London: Kegan Paul, Trench, Trubner & Co., Ltd., 1936), pp. 289-291.

[2]Porter, Arthur Kingsley, *Medieval Architecture, Its Origins and Development.* (New York: The Baker and Taylor Company, 1909), pp. 162-163.

[3]Many a modern tourist is puzzled and disturbed by the fact that the two spires of the west façade are not alike. Usually it has been thought sufficient, in explaining the incongruency, to point to the fact that they were built at widely different times—the one at the beginning of the thirteenth century, the other at

the beginning of the sixteenth—and to aver that each one was unselfconsciously built in the modern style of its own day. Yet plainly it was intended from the beginning that the two towers should not be identical. There are other irregularities in the façade: for example, neither the heads nor the feet of the royal figures are evenly aligned. It appears that the superintending architect was determined from the outset to design a façade that would manifest a measure of flexibility, so as not to confront the citizen with a legalistic and implacable schema.

The north spire, in Flamboyant Gothic, was begun in 1506—that is, on the eve of the Reformation, when various steps were being taken, during the papacy of Julius II, to strengthen the position of the church at a time when it was being subjected to severe criticism. The bishop of Chartres evidently thought it important that an effort should be made then to bring to completion the church that had remained obviously incomplete for three hundred years; but what he and his architect wanted to declare, it would seem, was their confidence in the possibility of *aggiornamento*—of renewing and updating the church, of showing that that institution could adjust itself to changing ideas and assimilate the new into the old. Even after the outbreak of the Reformation many leaders advocated a policy of accommodation, seeking to reconcile the differences between traditionalists and reformers. As it turned out, that party lost, in good part because of the intervention of Spanish conservatism at this point. We may be reasonably sure that if the second spire at Chartres had been built during the years of the Council of Trent (1545-1563) it would have been exactly like the first one.

[4]For an excellent study of the problem, see Panofsky, Erwin, *Renaissance and Renascences.* (Stockholm: Almquist & Wiksells, 1960.)

no word on Gothic in Spain or Germany and Germanic lands)

*Illustrations: F- 29
E- 5*

bibliography

AUBERT, M., and GOUBET, S., *Gothic Cathedrals of France and Their Treasures*. London: British Bk. Centre, Inc., 1959.

BECKWITH, J., *The Art of Constantinople*. New York: Phaidon Press, Ltd., Publishers, 1961.

——, *Early Medieval Art*. New York: Frederick A. Praeger, Inc., 1964.

BRANNER, R., *La Cathédrale de Bourges*. Paris: Tardy, 1962.

—— ——, *Gothic Architecture*. New York: George Braziller, Inc., 1961.

BUSCH, H., and LOHSE, B., editors (with introduction and commentaries on the illustrations by H. Weigert), *Gothic Sculpture*. New York: The Macmillan Company, 1963.

CLAPHAM, A. W., *English Romanesque Architecture After the Conquest*. New York: Oxford University Press, Inc., 1934.

CONANT, K. J., *Carolingian and Romanesque Architecture*. Baltimore: Penguin Books, Inc., 1959.

CRICHTON, G. H., *Romanesque Architecture in Italy*. London: Routledge & Kegan Paul, Ltd., 1954.

DEMUS, O., *Byzantine Mosaic Decoration*. Boston: Boston Book & Art Shop Inc., 1951.

—— ——, *Mosaics of Norman Sicily*. London: Routledge & Kegan Paul, Ltd., 1949.

DEWALD, E. T., *The Illustrations of the Utrecht Psalter*. Princeton: Princeton University Press (et al.), 1932.

DOWNEY, G., *Constantinople in the Age of Justinian*. Norman: University of Oklahoma Press, 1960.

DUPONT, J., *Gothic Painting*. New York: Skira, Inc., Publishers, 1954.

EVANS, J., *Art in Medieval France*. New York: Oxford University Press, 1948.

FOCILLON, H., *The Art of the West in the Middle Ages* (2 vols.). New York: Phaidon Press, Ltd., Publishers, 1963.

FRANKL, P., *The Gothic*, Princeton, N. J.: Princeton University Press, 1959.

GOUGH, M., *The Early Christians*. Frederick A. Praeger, Inc., 1961.

GRABAR, A., *Byzantine Painting*. New York: Skira, Inc., Publishers, 1953.

GRIVOT, D., and ZARNECKI, G., *Gislebertus, Sculptor of Autun*, New York: Orion Press, Inc., 1961.

HARVEY, J., *The Gothic World 1100-1600*. London: B. T. Batsford, Ltd., 1950.

— HINKS, R., *Carolingian Art*. London: Sidgwick & Jackson, Ltd, Publishers, 1935.

— KATZENELLENBOGEN, A., *The Sculptural Programs of Chartres Cathedral*. Baltimore: Johns Hopkins Press, 1959.

MACDONALD, W., *Early Christian and Byzantine Architecture*. New York: George Braziller, Inc., 1962.

— MÂLE, E., *The Gothic Image: Religious Art in France in the Thirteenth Century*. New York: Harper & Brothers, 1959.

⚬ MILLAR, E., *English Illuminated Manuscripts from the Xth to the XIIIth Century*. Paris and Brussels: Librairie nationale d'art et d'histoire, 1926.

NORDENFALK, C., and GRABAR, A., *Early Medieval Painting*. New York: Skira, Inc., Publishers, 1957.

⚬ OAKESHOTT, W., *The Sequence of English Medieval Art*. London: Faber & Faber, Ltd, 1950.

⚬ PÄCHT, O., *The Rise of Pictorial Narrative in Twelfth-Century England*. New York: Oxford University Press, 1962.

PEVSNER, N., *Outline of Architectural History*. Baltimore: Penguin Books, Inc., 1961.

— PORCHER, J., *Medieval French Miniatures*. New York: Harry N. Abrams, Inc., 1960.

— REINHARDT, R., *La Cathédrale de Reims*. Paris: Presses universitaires de France, 1963.

RICE, D. T., *The Art of Byzantium*, New York: Harry N. Abrams, 1959.

———, *Art of the Byzantine Era*. New York: Frederick A. Praeger, Inc., 1963.

———, *The Byzantines*. New York: Frederick A. Praeger, 1962.

⚬ RICKERT, M., *Painting in Britain: The Middle Ages*. Baltimore: Penguin Books, Inc., 1954.

— SAALMAN, E., *Medieval Architecture*. George Braziller, Inc., 1962.

SMITH, E. B., *The Dome, a study in the history of ideas*. Princeton: Princeton University Press, 1950.

— STENTON, F., *The Bayeux Tapestry*. London: Phaidon Press, Ltd, 1957.

STEWART, C., *The Byzantine Legacy*. London: Macmillan and Co., Ltd., 1947.

⇒ SUGER, Abbot of Saint Denis, *Abbot Suger on the Abbey Church of St. Denis and Its Art Treasures* (edited, translated, and annotated by E. Panofsky). Princeton, N. J.: Princeton University Press, 1946.

SWARZENSKI, W., *Monuments of Romanesque Art*. Chicago: University of Chicago Press, 1954.

SWIFT, E. H., *Hagia Sophia*. New York: Columbia University Press, 1940.

SYNDICUS, E., *Early Christian Art*. New York: Hawthorn Books, Inc., Publishers, 1962.

VOLBACH, W., *Early Christian Art*. New York: Harry N. Abrams, Inc., 1962.

— VON SIMSON, O. G.: *The Gothic Cathedral*. New York: Pantheon Books, 1956.

———, *The Sacred Fortress: Byzantine Art and Statecraft in Ravenna*. Chicago: University of Chicago Press, 1948.

WELLESZ, E., *The Vienna Genesis*. London: Faber & Faber, Ltd., 1960.

⚬ WORMALD, F., *The Benedictional of St. Aethelwold*. London: Faber & Faber, Ltd., 1959.

Pictures

→ France : 24

• England ; 6

= 24
= 6

index

From page 88
Popes from Cluny
Gregory VII
Urban II
Paschal II
From Clairvaux
Innocent II
Eugenius III

Cathedrals

France: Amien, Bourges, Chartres, Rheims; 4

England: Durham, Salisbury, York; 3

Italy: Orvietto, Pisa, Rome: 3

Germany: Worms, 1